W9-CHS-442

What Leaders Are Saying about *Supernatural Communication* and Rachel Hickson

"Intercessors should use this book as a manual to plan strategic prayer for their nations. In fact, every believer in every level of growth should read this book. The principles work and will change your life, family and nation."
—**Cindy Jacobs**, *cofounder, Generals International*

"A treasure trove on prayer. Rachel's spiritual understanding and insights are the outflow of a very close walk with Jesus. Every Christian should read and study this book."
—**Reinhard Bonnke**, *international evangelist*

"One of the most meaningful seasons of prayer at Covenant Church occurred during the ministry of Rachel Hickson as she led our congregation gently but brilliantly in a time of corporate prayer. Rachel, in her own inimitable way, skillfully guided hundreds of people into the throne room and taught us to listen for 'conversations' in the Godhead. We watched her do it; we did it together; and then we did it by ourselves. Those few remarkable hours that Rachel and her husband, Gordon, found to be with us were life changing, and I am convinced that any serious inquirer will discover in this book a way to pray that will be life transforming. I am eager to see this book in our bookstore and watch our church deepen in prayer as we embrace the principles Rachel so marvelously conveys."
—**Bishop Joseph L. Garlington Sr.**, *senior pastor, Covenant Church of Pittsburgh; presiding bishop, Reconciliation! Ministries International*

"Rachel Hickson is one of those unique and wonderful gifts to the Body of Christ. She is a woman who understands the Word and knows how to flow with the Holy Spirit. Rachel has the ability to minister into the lives of all people on every level. She reaches the broken, the young, the new convert and the mature saint. She has incredible depth in prayer and intercession, and her insights and inspiration will benefit any and all. I highly recommend Rachel and her ministry without hesitation."

—**Frank Damazio**, *senior pastor, City Bible Church, Portland*

"As a family we have greatly benefited from the insightful ministry of Rachel Hickson. It is one thing for prophetic ministries to speak generally into situations, but quite another to pinpoint issues beyond natural understanding. What we have found personally we have also experienced within the family of churches we represent. Rachel is biblical, connected to the local church and passionate in her desire to share the heart of the Father."

—**Stuart Bell**, *senior pastor, New Life Christian Fellowship, U.K.*

"I cannot think of anybody better equipped to write on this crucial subject. Rachel oozes passion for Jesus and outrageous faith."

—**Andy Hawthorne**, *CEO, The Message Trust*

"Rachel is a passionate preacher, evangelist, prophet and prayer warrior. Her gifts have been used to advance the Kingdom in many nations and her heart for the nations amazes me. But Rachel also has time for people and is kind, generous and fun."

—**Debra Green**, *Evangelical Alliance and City Links, Manchester, U.K.*

"Rachel is an anointed woman of God with a great heart for the Lord and His people. She has a clear prophetic gift and the ability to communicate profound spiritual truths in a simple and practical way. I am sure you will be blessed through this book."

—**Dave Smith**, *senior pastor, Peterborough Community Church, U.K.*

"Rachel Hickson has written an easy-to-read handbook for all who desire a fruitful prayer life, for prayer leaders looking for answers and for every would-be intercessor. She skillfully touches on all aspects of prayer sufficient to encourage even the new believer. *Supernatural Communication* should be used as a handbook to help churches establish prayer as a lifestyle. Our nation is dying for want of prayer;

a revolution in prayer lives is most desperately needed. May this book be used by the Lord to mobilize a praying army of those who will weep over our cities and nations until we see the arm of the Lord stretched out to heal and restore."
—*Eileen Vincent, founder, City Reachers for the Love of San Antonio*

"The books that have had the greatest impact on my life are those in which the author has something important to say, is able to write simply and clearly and, most of all, is writing things learned from the school of hard experience. Rachel Hickson and her book fulfill all these criteria. This book will make you long to have an effective prayer life and teach you exactly how to do it. Then it will teach you how to become an effective intercessor who can pray and get answers that have the power to change your world."
—*Alan Vincent, founder and president, Outpouring Ministries and Outpouring Missions International*

"We are living in the middle of a prayer awakening more widespread, deep and powerful than the world has ever seen. This is a strategic book that gives us steps to join in with what God is doing worldwide. God is using Rachel as a speaker who touches and moves the hearts of those who hear her. In this first book, she will touch, inspire and move to action the hearts of those who read. We are glad and privileged to have Rachel and Gordon Hickson working with us as part of our team in Oxford."
—*Charlie and Anita Cleverly, St. Aldates, Oxford, U.K.*

"Prayer can be so exciting and so hard! We all need encouragement, motivation and information to keep going. *Supernatural Communication* will supply that—and so much more, as it is full of practical advice borne out of a life of prayer."
—*Jane Holloway, National Prayer Director, World Prayer Centre, U.K.*

"It is my delight to endorse the ministry of Rachel Hickson. I believe she is one of the preeminent ministers in the Body of Christ today. Her emphasis and insights on prayer and intercession have impacted thousands around the world, including our own congregation. Rachel's prophetic preaching and teaching have

blessed our congregation time and again. With unusual candor, compassion and humor, this dynamic woman of God opens the Word of God in powerful and practical ways. Rachel's unusual combination of strengths—forceful, yet feminine; courageous, yet compassionate; dynamic, yet delightful—all serve to strengthen the Body of Christ, personally and corporately. Hear her, read her and receive her—your life will be the richer for having done so!"
—**Wendell Smith**, *senior pastor, The City Church, Seattle*

"Rachel Hickson is not only one of my heroes, but I am proud to say she is my mother, too. Watching her navigate her way through life and ministry has been inspiring. Her strength, integrity and genuine care of people have truly impacted me. I know that raising my brother, David, and me must have driven her to prayer on a daily basis! But there she tapped into the most amazing supernatural communication with God. Her life has been completely devoted to the plans and purposes that God has laid out for her, and there have been many sacrifices in becoming who she is today. But she is doing what she was born to do; she truly is a warrior princess."
—**Nicola Douglass**, *Hillsong Church, London*

"Rachel is a great encourager, combining prayer and pastoral care, and with a real heart for the transformation of people's lives and communities."
—**Joel Edwards**, *general director, Evangelical Alliance, U.K.*

"Rachel Hickson is the real deal—inspirationally passionate, eloquent and courageous, yet reassuringly warm, practical and down-to-earth as well. Rachel has journeyed through the valley of the shadow of death and is a walking, talking testimony to the supernatural power of prayer. Having appreciated Rachel's friendship, preaching and perspective, I am glad to commend her ministry and to endorse this book."
—**Pete Greig**, *founder, 24-7 Prayer*

Supernatural Communication

Supernatural Communication

How to Pray with Power and Authority

Rachel Hickson

Chosen

Grand Rapids, Michigan

© 2006 by Rachel Hickson

Published in the United States by Chosen Books
a division of Baker Publishing Group
P.O. Box 6287, Grand Rapids, MI 49516-6287
www.chosenbooks.com

• Published under the title *Supernatural Communication: The Privilege of Prayer*
by New Wine Ministries of West Sussex, England

Printed in the United States of America

All rights reserved. No part of this publication may be reproduced, stored in
a retrieval system, or transmitted in any form or by any means—for example,
electronic, photocopy, recording—without the prior written permission of the
publisher. The only exception is brief quotations in printed reviews.

           Library of Congress Cataloging-in-Publication Data
Hickson, Rachel.
     Supernatural communication : how to pray with power and
     authority / Rachel Hickson.
        p. cm.
     ISBN-10: 0-8007-9413-3 (pbk.)
     ISBN 978-0-8007-9413-2 (pbk.)
     1. Prayer—Christianity. I. Title.
     BV210.3.H53 2006
     248.3′2—dc22

                                                          2006046632

Unless otherwise indicated, Scripture is taken from the HOLY BIBLE, NEW
INTERNATIONAL VERSION®. NIV®. Copyright © 1973, 1978, 1984 by
International Bible Society. Used by permission of Zondervan. All rights
reserved.

Scripture marked NKJV is taken from the New King James Version. Copyright
© 1982 by Thomas Nelson, Inc. Used by permission. All rights reserved.

Dedication

I dedicate this book to three generations:

My parents, Alan and Eileen Vincent.
Who taught me to love Jesus and stirred in me the desire
to pray.

My husband, Gordon.
Who taught me to love intimacy and encouraged me
to press into prayer.

My children, Nicola and David.
Who motivated me to pray like never before and are
now amazing answers to the dreams of my heart!

Contents

Acknowledgments

There are a thousand different faces going through my mind at this moment that all deserve a thank-you! There has been an army of extraordinary people who have inspired and encouraged me to write this book. Thank you to my Heartcry team and the Watford, Hemel, Garston and St. Albans Community churches in Hertfordshire who walked the journey with me as we all learned to pray together. Thank you for praying and fasting for me to live in 1984!

Thank you to Reinhard Bonnke and the Christ for All Nations team for encouraging me and showing me an environment where prayer worked so quickly! It changed my life! Thank you to Tony Morton for trusting me when we returned to England in 1990 and encouraging me to preach—I never knew I would be a speaker until you gave me a platform. Thank you to Pastor Frank Damazio and the many churches in the United States who have opened your hearts to me and encouraged me to preach, teach and now write!

Thank you to my family who have paid a price as I have traveled but have always let me go with grace. Thank you for supporting me as I have written the manuals, done the teaching series and now edited the book. I love you and you are always my favorite people in the world and make me proud every day.

Thank you to Tim Pettingale who sent me an email about writing a book at the perfect time and has helped me every inch of the way. You have taken my work and made it a book, and I am so grateful for the hours and prayer you have given to this manuscript. You have done an outstanding job—thank you!

Finally, thank you for buying this book and I pray that it will change your life. I did not want to write just to have a book in print—I wanted to write so that somehow I could get the cry of this book written onto people's hearts! So thank you for walking this journey with me. Enjoy the read and then enjoy the life of Supernatural Communication!

Rachel Hickson
January 2006

Foreword

While there are a number of excellent books on the market on prayer, *Supernatural Communication* fills a need that none of them has touched. It is practical, funny, comforting and, most of all, human. You feel as if you have sat down across from Rachel with a cup of good English tea and enrolled in a "one-on-one" school of prayer.

Rachel has managed to achieve what few writers of non-fiction are able to do. She teaches with strong biblical understanding and puts her arguments in such a way that anyone, from a young child to a serious student of the Word of God, is able to learn.

The creative side of prayer that she touches on in chapter 2 answers questions that people may have had about this aspect of intercession but have been reluctant to ask. The Lord's children coming before Him to worship Him through dance and other creative arts, and at the same time releasing God's heart of intercession into the earth, is critical in this day.

Another important point Rachel makes about intercession is that spiritual warfare is for ordinary people. One does not have to be a five-star general to stand in the gap and see remarkable results. Some people are afraid to enter this realm, but Rachel makes it clear that we can and should do so—with the result of seeing the power of the enemy broken.

It also seems that Rachel has heard the heartbeat of God to delve into areas that are controversial to some in such a way that sets the record straight. She does an admirable job, for example, in her explanation of identificational repentance.

These are days of turmoil and violence, both in the natural and in the physical realms. If ever we needed a book like *Supernatural Communication*, it is today! I enjoyed it and was able to see things in a fresh light from the Holy Spirit as I read it.

Intercessors should use this book as a manual to plan strategic prayer for their nations. In fact, every believer in every level of growth should read this book. The principles work and will change your life, family and nation.

Great job, Rachel!

Cindy Jacobs
Generals International
Dallas, Texas

Supernatural Communication: The Privilege of Prayer

Introduction

There is a new sound penetrating the atmosphere—a new type of communication—the sound of passionate, praying people. Frequently, after I have finished speaking at a conference, people approach me asking, "Please will you train us? We want to be ready for action. We want to know how to pray effectively and still enjoy it." So, this book has been especially written for you! I really believe that the Holy Spirit wants to tutor you in His school of prayer, because God longs for you to connect with Him as never before.

Today God is looking for an army of ordinary people who will do extraordinary things. This is not a time for us to stand back and let the spiritual "superstars" take the lead, but this is a new season for ordinary men, women, grandparents, youth and children to go to the place of prayer together. These are exciting days! God wants each of us to build houses of prayer wherever we live so that we begin to see a radical transformation in the spiritual atmosphere of our neighborhoods, our cities and our nations. It is time for each one of us to arise and take our responsibility. These are urgent days and we need all hands on deck!

All over the world, prayer is taking a higher priority in people's lives than ever before. Now it is not uncommon for people to take time off from work in order to spend a day in focused prayer. In the past this would have been unheard of. In fact, even if you had offered to pay people to go to a church prayer meeting, they probably would have chosen to stay at home! But God is doing a new thing to raise the profile of prayer. All over the world there is a divine heartbeat—a call to prayer that is becoming so strong: "Come on, Church, now is the time to pray!" My prayer is that God will use this teaching to prepare your heart and to call you to this place of dedicated prayer.

Modeling a life of prayer

This heartcry is beginning to stir in God's people all over the world. People are saying, just like the disciples did, "Oh, Jesus, please teach me to pray."

In Luke 11:1 we read,

> One day Jesus was praying in a certain place. When he finished, one of his disciples said to him, "Lord, teach us to pray, just as John taught his disciples."

What was it that stimulated this question among the disciples? They had been watching Jesus pray and realized that after His times of prayer extraordinary miracles took place; they wanted to know how to have an overflow of power from their place of prayer just like Him! Jesus modeled the practice of prayer to His followers. Here is one of the most important things I want to highlight right at the beginning of this book: *If you want to teach and inspire others to pray, if you want to call others to intercession, you have to let them watch you pray!* Prayer should be contagious; we should catch it like a heavenly virus!

One of the reasons I love prayer is because my mom used to let me watch her pray. I remember as a little girl when she used to put me to bed, she would kneel at my bed once she had tucked me in, and with my mom's face next to mine, we would pray. I would hear her heart of prayer and feel the breath of her words across my cheeks and I knew God was listening. She taught me to pray by allowing me to see her doing it first.

Teaching people to pray is not just about giving them a manual! It's about inspiring them as they watch you pray! This is one of the major challenges we have in the Church. If we are not praying ourselves, then we can't teach others to pray. It's impossible to call others to come alongside you if you are not praying yourself! The public prayer life of the Church depends on the private prayer life of the leaders and individuals. But the exciting thing about what God is doing across our nations with increasing numbers of prayer rooms and initiatives such as 24-7 Prayer, is that these are providing an environment in which many more people can come and spend time with others who are modeling prayer. When people see authentic prayer modeled, they can begin to copy it. So much of prayer is caught and not taught. Leaders especially need to provide an environment where people can see them pray and say, "Wow! I want to learn to pray like that; I've *seen* you pray and I want to do it too."

When I think of Jesus and the incredible things He did— raising the dead; healing those who were blind, deaf, and dumb; speaking and silencing the weather patterns—I wonder what I would want Jesus to teach me? In the Church today we have a desperation to see such signs, wonders and miracles become common occurrences again. So if we were given the opportunity for a personal tutorial session with Jesus, what would we ask for? It is interesting that Jesus' disciples, who were with Him constantly and often saw Him moving in the supernatural, never asked Him, "Lord, teach us how to do miracles." The one specific area they wanted instruction on was *prayer*!

So I believe this must also be our first priority. We have got to really ask God to stir the desire to pray within us, so that we begin to ask Him, "Teach me, Jesus! I want to learn how to pray. Come alongside me, God. Teach me to love prayer."

Prejudices against prayer

Unfortunately, we have seen far too many stereotypes and held too many prejudices toward that word: *prayer*. Most of us, who have been brought up in church, remember the prayer meetings as boring. We remember those terrible sessions where people prayed for far too long and we had to find something with which to entertain ourselves to alleviate the boredom! It was either that or a great sense of relief came over us when we realized we had a date in our schedule that meant we could not attend the prayer meeting! For a long time that has been the attitude toward prayer, but God is busy redeeming prayer from its association with boredom! All over the world, people are finding that prayer can be an exciting and stimulating experience.

Prayer has often been connected with the word *failure*, too. There are those who feel that they have prayed and prayed but nothing has happened. Instead of prayer being a rewarding and fruitful exercise, for these people it has associations of disappointment and unfulfilled hopes. If this is you, God is wanting to renew your experience of prayer and help you to disassociate it from all those negative memories.

The individuality of prayer

I have already said that the cry of our hearts should be, "Oh, God, teach me to pray." If I were to add anything to that sentence it would be this: "Oh, God, teach me to pray in a style and with a language that is appropriate for me."

As we begin to train and call people into the place of prayer, we have got to recognize that the way in which each of us communicates is so individual. There is no perfect way to pray! There is no generic model of prayer that is perfect, but there *is* a perfect way for *you* to pray! Each person must settle on the style of prayer that is uniquely and perfectly *his* or *her* expression. Some people are very loud and demonstrative in their prayer and tend to do warrior-type praying. Others are much more meditative, contemplative and compassionate. Neither way is right or wrong—but together we can make a symphony of perfect prayer for our cities, communities and towns. You will only discover what your natural type of prayer is by doing it— you have to learn the language.

Each of us, then, must find the style of prayer appropriate for us. However, there will inevitably be seasons in prayer where everyone needs to shout. Even the quietest people will shout sometimes. Try stealing their purse or walking off with their wallet! They will shout to be heard! In the same way, in the place of prayer there are seasons when a certain type of prayer is called for. Sometimes it will be warrior-like warfare prayer, and other times it will be quiet, reflective prayer.

People often ask me, "How much should I be praying to have a real prayer life?" My answer is, "I haven't got a clue!" Why? Because I am not you! Do you see it? There is no formula for prayer. How often and how long you pray for depends on you and God! Don't think to yourself, *If I pray for five minutes about this, and five minutes about that and ten minutes about that . . . then I'll have it down.* Rather, forget the formula and just be yourself. There is nothing worse than trying to wear Saul's armor when you are a David.

Just as there will be loud and quiet seasons of prayer in your life, there will also be times when the demands of life govern how often and how long you pray. There will be times when God just comes upon you, and you may spend hours in prayer. But there will be other seasons in your life when it is not possible to do that—and that's okay! For instance, when you have a young baby, you will find that you are up during the night, your sleep will be disturbed, and you may be so busy that you only have five minutes here and there in which to pray. Maybe you previously had a season where you were able to pray regularly for two hours at the same time, but suddenly now you have a young child and you are grabbing time whenever you can. That is okay and it will not last forever—it is just a different season that will come and go. So many young mothers come to me depressed about this. "I think I'm backsliding," they say. I say to them, "Sweetie, if you are managing to pray at all, as well as feeding your baby and doing all the other things that need doing, then you are doing really well!" Do not be hard on yourself.

Prayer is not about filling a time slot, like you fill your time sheet for your work. So, simply ask the Holy Spirit, "Lord, teach me to pray in my season." As your life changes over the years, your seasons and patterns of prayer will change. Even in the space of a single year things can change—work pressures can come upon you if you own your own business; maybe suddenly you have the pressure of producing year-end financial statements, and so on. Does that mean, because your prayer life mainly consists of "Oh, God, help!" at that time, that suddenly you are backslidden? No! God knows that at that moment you need help, that's all! We need to feel comfortable in that because it really doesn't matter. Those who are prayer leaders and intercessors especially can get really condemned by this. "Help! I'm leading a prayer meeting and I haven't prayed much this week!" But it is not about that. It is about a heart that is running after God.

Of course, you cannot live forever on a wing and a prayer, so to speak! There do need to be those times when you pray more intensively, but you should not condemn yourself if you haven't always got it perfectly structured.

Developing a consistent personal prayer life

So how do we develop a consistent personal prayer life? I would like to give you a number of basic pointers that will help you to build a firm foundation for an effective and fulfilling prayer life.

Supernatural prayer needs to keep connected to intimacy

The bottom line is, prayer is about loving God. Prayer is a relationship. It is about getting online with an almighty God and staying connected. If it becomes a duty, a formula, or just "another 'to do' task in my busy life," then you have lost the connection. We all need to get past the idea that prayer is *another meeting* that we have to attend! Going to prayer meetings is just one small part of our prayer life. Prayer is much more about living a lifestyle of communication than that.

All around the world the advertising companies are telling us we need to get connected and at the same time there is a prophetic echo in the Church: "Get online with God and stay connected!" We understand that language today. We know it is essential to stay connected to the Web while we download information to our PC. In the Church there is a real cry for a supernatural breakthrough. We want to see God's power poured out in signs, wonders and miracles. So, if this is to happen through our prayer, then we had better stay connected while we download some power from heaven!

In fact, we must learn the secret of getting connected and staying online in order to receive the power of God we need for everyday life. We should be "downloading" whatever we need from the Holy Spirit all the time. God recognizes our frailty and knows that we need to constantly draw sustenance from Him.

Help, Lord! I feel weak

To that end, Romans 8:26 has become a very important Scripture for me. God has revealed it to me in so many different ways, and it has become one of my baseline Scriptures:

> In the same way, the Spirit helps us in our weakness.

I find it so comforting, that right here when the Bible is talking about this very important topic of prayer, God immediately says, "Don't worry! I know this is an area of weakness for you." God knows natural man is weak in the area of prayer. He knows exactly how we are wired! So many people say to me, "Rachel, I'm not really sure I'm a good pray-er. Maybe I shouldn't be involved in intercession because I struggle with it. I feel weak!" Anyone who is feeling like that, be encouraged, because right here the Holy Spirit says to you, "I know that!" In fact, God goes further and says to us, "That is *why* I've given you the Holy Spirit. He is there for you in your weakness." That is why we need this supernatural connection—because, naturally speaking, we are weak in this area, yet God has provided a wonderful answer to that weakness—the Holy Spirit.

Not knowing what to pray

Another common reason people give for not praying is not *knowing* what to pray for. Many people know that they should pray and even want to pray about certain situations that are important—and yet they don't pray because they can't find the right words. God has got this covered, too. Romans 8:26 continues,

> We do not know what we ought to pray for, but the Spirit himself intercedes for us with groans that words cannot express.

Think of the last time you heard a prayer request and thought, *I really ought to pray for that person, but I have no idea what to pray.* God's answer is that the Spirit Himself—not a substitute, but the Holy Spirit Himself—intercedes for us. Isn't that incredible? We need to come to a whole new place in our prayer lives where our praying is far more than mere words. Prayer is something supernatural! It is an event in which our spirit-man connects with the Spirit of God and something begins to come out of us that is supernatural. It's not just about us muttering some words. Every time we make that decision to connect to the Holy Spirit in the place of prayer, something supernatural happens that is beyond us. Although we feel weak and do not know what to pray, the Spirit Himself comes alongside us.

So God recognizes that we tend to be weak and also that we often do not know what we should pray. Consequently He has given us the Holy Spirit who desires to come alongside us and help us. Imagine, if you will, standing side by side with a friend so that your shoulders are touching. This is the image that Paul is seeking to convey to us: when the Spirit comes alongside you, you stand *shoulder to shoulder*. When that happens, it is not just about *me* anymore, it is about *us together*. Our shoulders are now jointly carrying the burden in the place of prayer. Where I am weak, He is strong; when I do not know what to pray for, He has surpassing knowledge. Together we can break through!

Every time you come to pray, I want you to take this picture with you: You are a *prayer team*, the Holy Spirit and you together—the most dynamic prayer partnership anyone has ever had. It is an incredible prayer combination. It is no longer about you on earth, desperately trying to connect with a big God "up there somewhere"—no! He has given you the Holy Spirit. He has come alongside you; the Helper is at hand. Every time you do not know how to pray, *the Spirit Himself* will complete your prayer. He will help you and direct you, and together you will make a successful prayer partnership.

Think of a situation in your life where you just do not know how to break through. Now pray, "Father, I believe that we are going to see a breakthrough in this situation, because You are going to help me pray. The Holy Spirit will give me the right words to pray."

Perhaps you think that when you connect with the Holy Spirit in this way, suddenly your prayers are going to sound so much more "professional." Maybe you will begin to sound really impressive because the Spirit is providing the vocabulary? No, Paul says that the Spirit will intercede for us with *groans that words cannot express*. I have discovered that the more I let the Holy Spirit into my prayer life, just the opposite has happened. My prayers have not become more polished at all. Rather, something deep is evoked from within that was not there before. It is like there is a new cry, a new desperation, a new hunger. Part of that groaning is that sometimes the Spirit begins to make you cry. You cannot even utter a word! But those very tears are powerful words of prayer. Often you will just feel something deep within you that goes beyond the possibility of translation into actual words—but that is prayer! It is not about the sound, it is about the spirit, and God is going to help you to develop that.

Sleeping on the job

Natural man is prone to sleep rather than pray! Even in a time of crisis, when perhaps the phone rings and someone sends through an urgent prayer request, it is difficult for us to stay focused. With every good intention we think, *Yes, I'm really going to pray for this person.* Maybe they are going to have major surgery the very next day, so you determine that you won't go to bed until you have prayed for them. You go and find a chair in a quiet room and determine that you are going to do business with God. Then an hour later you feel terrible as you wake up in the chair and realize you have been asleep the whole time!

Remember the story of the disciples in the Garden of Gethsemane (Mark 14:37)? We all judge the disciples for their lack of commitment, but if we are honest we have to admit we all have had friends in a crisis who have said, "Please watch and pray with me" and we have either forgotten or fallen asleep, haven't we?

In Gethsemane, when Jesus returned to His disciples, He found them sleeping. "Simon," He said to Peter, "are you asleep?" "No, no Lord, I was just meditating!" Peter might have replied. But of course he was fast asleep! "Can't you watch with Me for one hour?" Jesus asked. What is the answer to that? The honest answer is, no, natural man is not very good at that. Natural man cannot make it. The spirit is willing but the flesh is *really* weak. It is God who transforms our spirits, puts His heartcry within us and makes our spirits willing. Indeed, most of us have a real *willingness* to pray, but so often our bodies do not connect with our spirits. That is where the tension occurs, when our bodies fail to come into line with the inner desires of our spirit.

So how do we overcome that tension? Again God has provided an answer. We call in the Holy Spirit: "God, I want to pray, but I have to confess that my body is still weak. I tend to sleep and forget to pray. Holy Spirit, please come alongside me and help me." Whatever you do, do not allow yourself to be driven into depression or condemnation. Your situation is not unique—every single one of us has the tendency to be sleepy and forgetful in our prayer lives. Rather, let this weakness drive you into a desperation for the Person of the Holy Spirit to help you.

The divine adapter

In teaching about prayer, I often use the illustration that the Holy Spirit is like an "adapter" that helps us align correctly to our heavenly power source. I travel a lot and one of my challenges is that my electrical equipment doesn't adapt as easily as I do! If I want to plug my hairdryer in, for instance, it often won't fit into the electrical outlet. What do I need? An adapter. I see the Holy Spirit like that. Often I come to pray and I want to get connected with the supernatural, almighty God. I begin to express myself, but somehow I know that the words coming out of my mouth do not make the complete connection of all that I sense in my spirit. I need divine help to adapt my language, and I have the Holy Spirit for this. He comes and He takes my heartcry, He takes my words, He takes who I am, and He adapts it to connect it with almighty God. To express your prayer effectively, you must keep plugging in to the Holy Spirit. He is your adapter.

Another thing I have noticed when I travel is that there are different ratings of power supplies in different nations. Although the Americans may not like to admit this, the British do have more power than them! The British have a 240-volt power supply while the Americans have a 110-volt supply. So, whenever I am in the United States, even though I am using my adapter to plug my hairdryer into the outlet, when I turn on the power to dry my hair it sounds very slow and sick! It needs a lot more power to make it work effectively. It is the same with us. We get connected and we begin to talk to God, but the prayer that comes out of our mouths sounds underpowered. We think, *How is this prayer ever going to heal my friend with cancer or raise the dead? God, I wanted to pray a "big" prayer because I have a big problem. I need more power!* So we need to let the Holy Spirit take our words and transform them to make them powerful for the pulling down of strongholds, and He is more than willing to do this because He understands and is fully aware of our own weakness and inability.

We need to hold this picture of prayer once again. It is not just about you; it is about your prayer being connected to the transformer of the Holy Spirit. Now your prayer can be powerful. All the books you read, the seminars you attend, or whatever else you use to help you get into the place of prayer are wonderful, but it is actually *this connection* that is going to transform your prayer life.

We need to become a friend of Jesus

As well as needing the Holy Spirit to come alongside us to help us to pray, we need to become a friend of Jesus—because prayer is a relationship with a Person. Friendship will keep your passion for prayer alive. It is a two-way street of communication. Prayer is about knowing that as you touch the heart of God, God is going to touch your heart.

I was thinking recently about how the entire Bible is the story of a great romance. It is the original romantic love story where a bridegroom (the Prince of all princes) falls in love with a princess (the bride of the earth) and wants to marry her. Eventually the day of the great wedding comes, the bride and bridegroom are perfectly united and they live happily ever after in the presence of an almighty King! It is an incredible love story of epic proportions!

Lost friendship

But let us pause for a moment and think about the beginning of this great story—when God created Adam and Eve and placed them in the beautiful Garden of Eden. God and man enjoyed wonderful fellowship for a time, until the fateful Fall occurred, recorded in Genesis 3. However, whenever we teach about the Fall of man, what do we emphasize? We teach and concentrate on what *we* lost in the Fall. We teach about how we lost perfection, how we fell into sin, how we lost our place in the garden, how we lost our relationship with the Father. But as I was reading this passage one day, God suddenly said this to me: *"Rachel, have you ever thought about what I lost that day?"*

Have you ever thought about what God lost when we sinned in the garden? As I thought about it that day, it made me cry. Do you know what God lost? He lost friendship. God and Adam often walked and talked together in the garden, enjoying one another's company. In Genesis 3:8–9 we read that God is walking once again in the garden, looking for Adam. Having sinned, Adam and Eve hear God coming and hide from Him. So the Lord calls out, "Where are you?" Can you hear that cry? Since God spoke to me about this passage, I no longer hear that cry as one of an irritated parent looking for an errant child; I hear a cry of anguish as God realizes that He has lost His friendship and what it will take to restore it. Since that day, God's cry has never changed. There is in the earth the incredible cry of a friend and Father calling for mankind, "Where are you?" because we were created for relationship and communication.

That is why God the Father sent His only begotten Son. That is why the Bridegroom of heaven offered to lay His life down. Why? He did this because it was the only way that this communication gap could be restored and closed. The Father desired that the veil be torn in two so that every man, woman and child could become connected to Him in relationship once again. The heartcry of God has always been *friendship*. He says, "I want to know you." From the least to the greatest He wants to know us—heart to heart. He is calling you to relationship.

The lie of fear and inadequacy

> But the LORD God called to the man, "Where are you?"
> He answered, "I heard you in the garden, and I was afraid because I was naked; so I hid."
>
> Genesis 3:9–10

Adam's reply to the Father reveals a lie that the devil has sold us for so long—that we are completely inadequate and for that reason ought to be afraid of talking to God. This is the very first place we read about fear in the Bible and it is linked with communication. So often we have bought that lie and been frightened to talk to God. The devil, again and again, has condemned our prayer lives. Do you ever feel that your prayer life is just not good enough? You always feel that you do not do it right, that you do not have the right words? God so desires to have intimate communication with us that the enemy will do whatever he can to thwart it. God wants you to talk to Him, so the enemy constantly whispers to you, "Don't talk! Your prayers are pathetic. No one is going to listen to you. You're irrelevant. You can't say it right!" Yet, the cry of God has never changed: "Where are you? I want to talk with you."

The enemy will use any kind of intimidation he can to shut us up so that we do not talk to God. He wants to stop us from talking and expressing ourselves. His tactics have not changed since that first time in the garden. So we must come to God with a fresh determination and say, "Father, I am going to break every bit of intimidation, every bit of fear, off my life. I am going to be a determined communicator with almighty God. I am going to be connected."

God is calling you to meet with Him face-to-face. Have you ever spoken to someone face-to-face, quite close together? It can be intimidating at first. You have to become a little bit vulnerable because you have to look the person directly in the eyes. That is the kind of communication that God wants with you—looking into one another's eyes and being completely transparent. That is why one of the enemy's key tactics is to put as much guilt, shame and condemnation on you as he possibly can. Why? Because guilt, shame and condemnation cause you to hang your head! Once you are weighed down by guilt, you are no longer looking into God's eyes.

We must come to such a new understanding of the truth that God has completely delivered us from all of our sin. You need to know just how thoroughly and utterly God has forgiven you. When you know that you are forgiven, then you can walk with your head up and shoulders back into the presence of God—not with any sense of arrogance, but with the confidence of knowing who you are in Christ. He has forgiven you and you can know that the eyes of the Bridegroom look on you with incredible love. You can look Him in the eyes and know that you bring Him satisfaction and friendship.

You bring pleasure to God

In the first chapter of the book of Song of Songs, the bride sees herself as being entirely inadequate for the bridegroom. She says, in effect, "Don't look at me! I'm dark . . . I'm ugly . . . I'm small-breasted. . . . " But by the end of Song of Songs it seems as though the persistent love of the bridegroom has completely changed her identity. She sees herself in a new light and is saying, "I am full-breasted and I bring him great contentment." Her identity has been healed in the presence of God. Not only has the bridegroom given her something, but she now knows that she also has something to give. Throughout the Bible the breast is a picture of provision and nourishment, and this is what is being portrayed here.

We all must come to the revelation that we give pleasure to God. In response to the very heartcry of God that says, "Where are you?" we can walk into His presence and say, "Father, here I am! I am here for you." Something rejoices in the heart of God when you do that. The very fact that you have taken the time to be in His presence brings Him joy. As you spend time with our incredible God, and talk to Him in conversation (which we tend to call *prayer*), He will talk to you more and more (which we tend to call *revelation* or *the prophetic*). As you spend time with God, He will spend time with you, too! You will find yourself having dreams, revelations, even prophetic words, as your communication with the Father becomes more intimate. This is the natural outworking of a two-way conversation with God.

Good prayer depends on relationship

Good prayer is always going to depend on your relationship with God. I love the Scripture John 15:15, which says, "I no longer call you servants, because a servant does not know his master's business." The relationship of a servant to his master reflects the "religious" relationship. It is a relationship in which you are performing a role often out of a sense of duty. In such a relationship you might come to God and "report back" saying, "Yes, Lord, I've done this ... I've done that ... I've earned my points and now I need You to help me. I have been a good servant." You could call that a relationship of sorts, but it depends entirely upon your ability to perform. You have done your duty. That is what a servant does. But God does not want us to be "human doings," He wants us to be "human beings," able to have a true relationship with Him and become His friend. We can approach God on an entirely different basis, knowing that He is a friend who longs to share His heart with us. God doesn't just want to give you a job and relate to you as the boss—He loves you and wants to give you His heart and relate to you as your friend.

The next part of the Scripture hits me time and again. "Instead, I have called you friends, for *everything* that I learned from my Father I have made known to you" (emphasis added). Isn't that incredible? Just think about that: Jesus is saying that everything He has learned from His Father in that secret place of intimate communion—all of that He wants to make known to you. That is how much God wants to reveal to you. How much do you want?

We all know that really good friendships take time. If you are prepared to put the time into a relationship, then eventually you will be rewarded with a more intimate knowledge and understanding of that person. If you give time, then you will receive information. I want to encourage you to spend time with God and to expect, as a result, that He will open the windows of heaven and allow you to see and understand things that were previously unseen. There are whole areas in which I am currently knocking on the door of heaven saying, "Lord, I want the information download to be able to see signs, wonders and miracles happen in our nation." Such revelations will not be given without spending the time in God's presence, talking with Him.

We all understand that if we want to download large files from the Internet we have to be online a longer time than if we are just checking a short message. It is the same with prayer. If you want to have access to greater depths of heavenly knowledge, you need to stay connected and online for longer periods of time. God wants to share with you the secrets of heaven, but will you take the time to listen and download the information? Will you carve time out of your day to become a friend of God? So often we are just crisis friends; we only seek the face of God when our life is tough and we need help, but I believe that God wants us to be consistent friends that are available for Him even when we do not need an answer for our personal lives. We need to have a two-way friendship and become a faithful friend that enjoys talking with Him even when we feel fine!

Simple prayer works

In these days we need to have far more confidence that simple prayer works. Have you ever just cried out, "Oh, God, help!" and received a miraculous answer? At other times we can struggle and labor in the place of prayer without seeing any results and think, *Oh, the problem is I'm just no good at prayer.* But then, we decide just to cry out to God, almost incoherently, and boom! He answers! Sometimes with all our training, knowledge and information we can lose our simplicity. Effective prayer does not have to be complicated. Essentially, good prayer is about you being relaxed and just being yourself in the place of prayer, confident of your relationship with Him. You do not need to impress God with your eloquence! Simple prayer does work.

Feeling too small to pray?

So often we choose to focus on ourselves and our inabilities rather than on God and His abilities. "I don't think I can pray for that because I'm not big enough.... I don't have enough faith.... I can't find the right words." But prayer is all about how big God is! Thank goodness it does not depend on how great or small we feel we are.

Something that had a profound effect on me, and amply illustrates this point, was seeing a little girl praying for the sick in Africa. My husband, Gordon, and I were working with Reinhard Bonnke and we had an associate evangelist with us, Kenneth Meshoe, who had an amazing healing ministry. Kenneth's daughter, who was about four years old at the time, tagged behind him, constantly hanging onto his pant legs as he prayed for literally hundreds of people at a time. Everyone's eyes were on the "big evangelist," but following behind him, praying for every person, would be this little girl who only came up to people's knees! Kenneth would pray for each person and move on and then came his daughter, copying her dad.

Often after the little girl had finished praying, the person would exclaim, "I can see! I can hear!" and so on. Onlookers would no doubt have attributed the healings to Kenneth's ministry, but I often wondered to myself, was it the prayers of this little girl that God had answered? Simple prayers work!

Often when we are faced with a big problem, we think we need to have a big answer. No! Just be yourself. Let the prayers come naturally, simply, and God will hear and answer. We all have our own style in prayer. Some people pray very emotionally with much compassion and tears; some are much more warrior-like and militant in their prayer; others still are very quiet and reflective, communicating with God in apparent silence. Which way is more effective? There is not a more or a less effective way—it has just got to be genuine. Sometimes there will be a situation that will trigger many tears; other times there will be the sound of incredible warfare. We need to be sensitive to the Spirit and let Him orchestrate the sound of our prayer. There will be times when you will not pray according to your style of personal preference, but just let the God-sound be released from your heart. Remember, simple, sincere, honest prayer is what is important. I felt God say to me once, "Simple prayers from a hungry heart will reach the heart of God." I couldn't put it better.

Sincere prayers touch God's heart

I grew up in India as a little girl. My father was a minister in Bombay Baptist Church and we lived above the church. On one particular Sunday, I was around four and a half years old at the time, my father was downstairs conducting the evening meeting and a lady from the church was putting me to bed. As she was doing so, I turned to her and said, "Please, can I have Jesus in my heart?" Reportedly, this was my prayer: I took hold of my pillow, hugged it very tight and said, "Dear Lord Jesus, I want You to be as close to me for the rest of my life as my pillow is right now." It worked!

We do not need to pray long, complicated prayers, and our prayers do not always have to be for deeply spiritual things. Don't you find yourself praying for parking spaces? I think in Britain we are very good at this, as there just don't seem to be enough to go around! We even trained our children to do it for us! I remember, when my kids were very young, they would even argue, "No! It's my turn to pray for the parking space!" God did not seem to mind their arguments and He still provided the parking spaces!

I feel I cannot emphasize enough that God is the God of the individual. He is the micro and the macro God, able to hold both vast infinity and personal individuality in perfect tension. Your uniqueness is so precious to Him. He is intimately acquainted with your personality with all its idiosyncrasies. Because of that, He wants to have a personal conversation with you, not just mere religious repetition. So when you pray you need to remember that God loves people, all types of people, and make sure that your prayers do not become pharisaical and critical of others. Remember, God loves them, too!

In Luke 18:9–14 we read the well-known parable that Jesus told about a Pharisee and a tax collector. It says that,

> To some who were confident of their own righteousness and looked down on everybody else, Jesus told this parable: "Two men went up to the temple to pray, one a Pharisee and the other a tax collector. The Pharisee stood up and prayed about himself: 'God, I thank you that I am not like other men—robbers, evildoers, adulterers—or even like this tax collector. I fast twice a week and give a tenth of all I get.'
>
> "But the tax collector stood at a distance. He would not even look up to heaven, but beat his breast and said, 'God, have mercy on me, a sinner.'
>
> "I tell you that this man, rather than the other, went home justified before God. For everyone who exalts himself will be humbled, and he who humbles himself will be exalted."

Good prayer has more to do with your heart attitude than with your verbal language. Do not pray from a position that sounds like you have got life sorted out, asking God to please sort out the other person. Remember, even if your life seems all together in this season, this is only because of the goodness of God to you. Be careful when you pray to keep an attitude of gratitude concerning the generosity of God in your life. Remember that if God did not help you with your marriage, your children and your life, you would be facing many difficulties. Do not pray from an exalted position that sounds like this: "Thank You, God, that our marriage is good and our kids are not on drugs and our daughter is not pregnant..." but pray with a heartfelt compassion that understands the pain of others' lives. Keep it simple and do not judge people when you pray.

Specific prayer works

Often we hesitate to really focus our prayers on a specific target. But if you aim at nothing, then you will usually hit it! Too often our prayers are vague and directionless. We don't really know what we are expecting and so we pray very general prayers without specific purpose. People often tell me that they have been praying for years, but my question is, "What have you been praying for?" People tend to pray "blanket" prayers. "I've been praying for God's blessing," they say. But what is the specific area you are asking God to bless? "Well, I have been asking God to bless my marriage," they might reply—but what specific area of your marriage needs the blessing of God? Do you want God to bless your communication, your finances or another area of your marriage? Unless you are specific with your requests to God, how do you know when they have been answered? We all need the encouragement of answered prayer to be persistent in our prayer lives, and so we need to be able to identify and quantify the results of our prayers.

To begin with, you could set yourself a personal monthly prayer target. In addition, you could have a longer-term goal that you want to see come to pass in that year. Some time ago I visited a church in America that set a different prayer goal as a corporate target each new year. This particular year the church members felt God leading them to set the goal of seeing the mortgage paid off on their church property. As a group of believers they were praying for this and obviously giving toward it, too, as God blessed their personal finances. By the end of that year their debt had been completely settled.

So I asked them, "What is your goal for this next year?" and they said that God had told them, because they had honored Him by settling the debt on His house, He now wanted them to pray about their personal debts and see what He would do. So they began to gather together the information and quantify what was the collective debt of the church members. They placed a basket at the front of the church so that they could begin to pray and address each specific need. At first the basket was full of many papers with various information, but as each debt was completely paid, the papers were removed from the basket, so that they could literally watch the level decrease as their prayers were being answered.

That is exactly what we need to do. When we have a prayer need, whether great or small, we need to identify and specifically pray for it. So I encourage you, make sure that your prayer life has specific goals, so you can look and say, "Yes, I can see God answering my prayers." I recognize that there may be some areas of your prayer life in which you can't be so specific, but where you can, you should have definite goals.

Children are very good at praying specific prayers. Once my son, David, really wanted to go skiing, so he began praying that he would get an opportunity to go in the near future. Before long we received an invitation to minister in Norway over the New Year period after Christmas. The conference was to be held at a hotel. When David heard of the invitation, he immediately asked, "Do they have skiing there?" I told him that I thought they did. Further investigation revealed that this particular hotel adjoined one of the best ski resorts in Norway! David said, "That's it! You don't need to pray about this invitation. This is God!" Bless him! He had been calling in the skiing holiday that he desperately wanted, and here it was! Maybe you think that is a rather audacious way to pray? God did not seem to care. He answered David's prayer anyway.

Our son, David, was born in Kenya. But he was still very small when we moved back to England and so did not really remember much about his birthplace. Because of this he wanted to return and visit "his" land. Gordon and I thought about saving regularly so that we could send him to Kenya for his eighteenth birthday. David said that was fine, but began to pray about it. Three days later my parents came around to visit and my mom said, "Can I talk to you for a minute?" She took me to one side and said, "We are going to Kenya in April and we just felt that maybe we should take David with us. What do you think?" I said, "Well, David was only just praying about that a few days ago! Do you want to speak to him?" We called David down from his room to come and have a private word with his grandparents. Moments later he emerged from the room exclaiming, "Yes! That's much better than having to wait years to save up the money!" My children, probably more than anyone, have taught me about being specific in prayer.

Being specific in prayer applies not just to our personal needs, but also for the needs of others—even whole communities. All of us who are involved in the London Prayernet are seeking to pray specific, focused prayers—we are not simply praying, "God bless London." We are knocking on the doors of members of Parliament, local counselors and educators, asking, "Will you tell us exactly what your needs are? We want to pray strategically and specifically. We want to know that we are praying where the community is hurting." As we have done that, we have seen some wonderful answers to our prayers.

A group of pastors in the London borough of Haringey decided to find out what the prayer needs of their community were and engage in focused prayer in order to see some quantifiable results. These pastors have seen many answers to prayer across the borough. Their community had many schools that were failing. In the United Kingdom, schools that are underperforming tend to have their government subsidies cut and so their annual budgets can become smaller and smaller as a result. It is incredibly disheartening as the already failing school becomes further underresourced and fails even more.

When the pastors visited the school authorities they were asked to pray for a significant improvement in the schools' performance and a corresponding increase in funding. So they prayed specifically over the next nine months that there would be a turnaround. Schools in England are rated in a national performance table and during this year, the schools' ratings moved from minus eight to plus seven! As a result, Haringey council sat up and noticed what these pastors were doing! Now the council faxes and emails the pastors with specific prayer requests on a regular basis!

We need to have compassion and warfare in the place of prayer

Just as God's wrath and God's compassion are two facets of the same perfect Father, so God wants us to represent these "two faces" of His character in the place of prayer—the face of the lion against the enemy in warfare, and the face of the lamb in compassion toward the lost and needy. Unfortunately, in the Church we often get the face of the lion and the lamb confused. We roar like a lion against other people, but then act like a lamb toward the devil. God wants that reversed. He wants the Lion of Judah to thwart all of the devil's schemes, but the Lamb of God to show compassion and mercy to all those who have been brutalized by the enemy. We need both attitudes in prayer. Just as we see war and weapons being used to remove the dictators in the world, we need to engage in spiritual warfare, but equally we then need to take compassion and mercy to those who have suffered. *Prayer carries all the resources to rebuild the people of the land.*

God is calling His Church back to the place of serious prayer and intercession. I always say that *the prayer of intercession is the prayer of generosity.* Why? Because it is prayer that you give away. People tend to think, *Well, I'm not an intercessor. I can't pray for hours and hours on end—that's not my calling.* Intercession isn't only about that. Every man, woman and child is called to be an intercessor, because at its heart, intercession is simply about being like Jesus. Intercession is the prayer that stands in the gap; it is the prayer that builds the bridge of hope to the unreached; it is prayer that goes beyond the "me, myself and I" comfort barrier and begins to share the concerns of God. God looks at your city, the streets and alleys and those who walk there and He is concerned. We need to respond to Him by saying, "Yes, God, I will carry Your heartcry; I will listen to Your prayer request." Intercession is praying from God's prayer-request list. It is choosing to be a prayer partner with Him.

Isaiah 62:10 says,

> Pass through, pass through the gates!
>   Prepare the way for the people.
> Build up, build up the highway!
>   Remove the stones.
> Raise a banner for the nations.

God is looking for people who will bridge the gap and *prepare a way* for people to come to God. As intercessors we need to build a highway that will bring people into contact with the living God. Every prayer we pray is like a bit of asphalt on that road. There is a gap between God the Father and the person or situation you are praying for. Intercession has to stand in that gap. We cannot lay the entire highway in one sitting, but we can keep revisiting it, coming back to lay another square yard. We keep praying until we see a highway established that connects that person or situation to the Father. We are the bridge, the intermediary. We need to remember that even when we cannot seem to see any results, something is being built. *Praying time is never wasted time*. Each time we pray, something is happening and a highway is being built in the spiritual realm. One day it will break through and be seen in the natural realm and you will see your answer. So remember, do not give up! Keep praying and build the highway of prayer and see what answer will walk across your life because you took time to pray for someone else!

We need to expect joy and satisfaction

I expect to thoroughly enjoy the place of prayer. Prayer has a reward of joy and does not need to be all toil and hard work. The Church needs to redeem the place of prayer as a place of incredible joy. Isaiah 56:7 says, "These I will bring to my holy mountain and give them joy in my house of prayer." As you begin to spend more and more time in the place of prayer, God is going to take you on a journey. He wants to take you up onto the mountaintops with Him, to a place of intimacy, and He wants to give you incredible, outrageous fun and joy in the house of prayer. Isaiah continues, "Their burnt offerings and sacrifices will be accepted on my altar" (Isaiah 56:7). It costs us something to pray; there is going to be some sacrifice; there are going to be some tough times. Occasionally prayer *will* feel like hard work. It takes discipline and sacrifice, but you can take that discipline and lay it as an offering on the altar. God's response to you will be, "I'm going to accept it all. For My house will be called a house of prayer for all nations." Expect a new season of enjoyment. God is going to give you joy in the house of prayer.

Creative Prayer: Types and Styles of Prayer

Building a creative house of prayer—one that resembles you!

All around the world God is stirring in His people the desire to have a consistent, satisfying prayer life. Most people sense that *now* is the time to pray. Many even have the desire and passion to pray, but somehow find their discipline still fails. They make their plans to pray with great regularity, but soon find they fail as their prayer life seems so sterile and unproductive. They find their prayer time becomes sleeping time, not speaking time! In this chapter I want to look at some types and styles of creative prayer that I hope will help you to break out into new levels of communication in your prayer life.

At the end of the previous chapter, we read in Isaiah 56:7 that God wants to give us "joy in my house of prayer." I want you to think about that image of "building" a *house of prayer*, because building a solid prayer relationship is like renovating and decorating a house. Maybe it is easier for me to imagine this because I am a woman, but what does every woman want to do when she moves into a new house? She wants to change it, paint it and renovate it. Why? Because she wants to put her stamp on it. She wants to make it *her* house. Hold that thought in your mind as we look at how each one of us can build our personal house of prayer.

When establishing our prayer life we often adopt other people's models of prayer too quickly. We copy their ideas and methods, assuming they will work for us, when we should really be finding our own style and routine of prayer with God. People have often asked me, "Rachel, how long should I pray to have a *real* 'quiet time'?" My answer is: I don't know! How long do *you* think it should be? Maybe it shouldn't even be called a "quiet time"—it might be better for you to have a noisy time! If you ask me what constitutes a really good time of prayer, my answer to you will be, "Well, what are the things you love to talk about? What really interests you?" Who are you and how has God made you to function? Your interests, passion and vision will all determine what is right for you.

In these days I believe God is restoring a freedom, individual expression and style back into the place of prayer just as He has done and is doing in our corporate worship. In the past, much of our worship was very structured, orchestrated and defined, but now the Holy Spirit has breathed into it and begun to loosen it up. He has encouraged us to express ourselves more freely and has inspired new songs and new sounds. Now we usually have a band with drums and other instruments, not just an organ or a piano playing hymns, and our music and rhythm have changed. Similarly with our prayer lives, God wants to take us outside of the box in which we have lived for so long.

God once said to me regarding prayer, *It's time to color outside the lines.* God is a God of principles and that's why He gives us instructions—boundaries within which we should function. But there is a sense in which the color of God splashes outside the actual principle sometimes, because after all they are not *rules*, they are *principles*. A rule says, if you step over this line you're dead! But a principle is different—it is a *guide* and with guides there are always pros and cons to consider. For example, on principle I would make sure I put my kids to bed before 8:00 P.M. most nights when they were under ten years old, but if family came to visit or it was a special occasion, we colored outside the lines, and the children went to bed late! As you read this chapter, remember that I am trying to give you principles, not rules—principles that I hope will help you to build the basic structure of your house of prayer. But remember the final décor is yours; everyone's house will be different, because this is *your* adventure.

God wants you to be creative in your prayer life. You are the architect of your house of prayer and you are creating a habitation for a relationship with almighty God. Isn't that fantastic? You are building something that is personal to you and that welcomes Jesus in.

Prayer is a lifestyle, not just something you put in your schedule to do on a Wednesday morning or whenever. All of us need to live with the sense that we are ready to communicate with the living God at any time, to be connected to Him in such a way that He is involved with every area of our lives. In other words, to welcome Him into every room in our house—no room is out of bounds.

God wants you to have a lifestyle of prayer that means you are in constant touch with Him, talking about everyday needs and even the most mundane of things. But He also wants you to have times of focused intimacy with Him. Prayer on the run is fine, as long as there are "deep contact" times, too. A healthy prayer life is like a healthy marriage: It is possible to go about life busily, keeping in touch by cell phone and getting on with things, but you also need time alone, just the two of you, with no interruptions. In your prayer life there needs to be times where it is just you and God, sitting opposite one another, face-to-face, heart-to-heart, and you talk.... I call these times of intimacy with God "Table for Two" time! You need to have the mixture of good, general administrative communication with personal, intimate communication for a good marriage, and it is the same with prayer. If you think about it in those terms, then you are saying to God, "This is the time when I want to set a place just for You. There's nobody else, just You and me. No other pressures will intrude on our time together." That creates a whole different atmosphere. Then your "quiet time" can no longer be a quick "ten minutes" before you rush out the door.

Before someone interprets me as saying really long quiet times *are* essential, let me say this: Some people are almost superstitious about having a quiet time and that attitude totally misses the point. I have even heard people say, "I had a crash in my car this morning. Someone ran into the back of me. It must have been because I cut short my quiet time!" I do not think that is why! You cannot be superstitious about prayer because prayer is a conversation with a friend. Do you think that God would vindictively slam a car into the back of you because you only said a quick "Hi" to Him this morning? No! The important thing to remember is that all prayer is about connectedness based in relationship.

Let me ask you a question now. When was the last time you set a Table for Two and made a date with God? When was the last time you came to God just for Him? Not because of your crisis or your needs, but because of who He is? God wants to have time with you with no personal agendas getting in the way. I believe this is why so many retreat centers have sprung up in recent years. It is as if God is saying, "Come away with Me, let's spend time together." We usually are not too good at giving this kind of attention to God at home because there are too many distractions. The phone will ring and we will think,

I'll just get this and then carry on praying afterwards. Most of us discover praying time is never a convenient time!

All of us need to get away and spend time alone with God, but this is especially true for leaders. Ministers will begin to come to God's Word more often than not, looking to receive something they can give away to others. It takes a significant adjustment in the mind of a leader to come to God's Word just for himself or herself. All leaders need times when they can take off their ministry "hats" and just come as themselves before God; come to Him not because of their responsibilities in the church, but as a child. (I call these two facets "ministry Rachel" and "little Rachel.") Developing this discipline can take time and often a changing of our mindsets. If you are a leader, then think about taking three or four days away at regular intervals to set work aside and just sit in God's presence to talk things over and receive from Him for yourself.

Positions of prayer

So once you have decided to have some Table for Two time with God, what do you do? How do you pray? What tools will help you to build a house of prayer? In the latter section of this chapter I want to discuss several distinct types of prayer, but before that I would like to consider some different positions for prayer that I hope will be helpful to you.

Standing up

The way in which you position your body says a lot about how you are going to communicate. We are taught this even in business. If you walk into an office and both people stand up, that says something. If you walk into an office and the other people remain seated at their desk, that says something different. Often people will stand because they want to be on equal terms with the other person or to give an atmosphere of honor. Remaining seated can often be a nonthreatening sign meaning, "You are welcome here" and does not carry the same sense of threat. Standing in God's presence to pray can be a very positive posture: It releases a sense of honor—I stand in awe of You! Or it can be indicative of a warrior attitude.

Sitting down

There is a place for the standing warrior prayer, but there is also a place for sitting in God's presence. This is a time when we are more receptive, waiting upon God and listening to hear what He will say to us. Just this change of position will alter the way in which you communicate.

Kneeling

Kneeling is a prayer position that immediately puts things into perspective: big God, little you. We need to remind ourselves often of the vast majesty of God balanced with the fact that He is our Father and we need to surrender to Him as He guides and directs our lives. Kneeling is a good way of reminding ourselves that we are dependent upon Him and acknowledging His care. I bow before You, almighty God.

Prostrate

Sometimes it is good to simply lie down in God's presence. Someone once said to me, "I've developed a new posture for prayer. I lie in His presence and say, 'You're a great big God; take it all!' " Whenever you are overwhelmed with weariness, lie in God's presence and say to Him, "I acknowledge that You are a big God; You are great; You are mighty." There is something very wonderful about just lying in the Father's presence like that. Remember, He makes me lie down in green pastures!

Driving

Can you drive a car and pray at the same time? Yes, but preferably not with your eyes closed! You don't always have to pray with your eyes shut. I learned to increase my frequency in tongues while I was driving. I would look at the clock and say to myself, *Okay, now I'm going to pray in my prayer language and build up my spirit-man for five minutes.* Then I would just talk in my heavenly prayer language. At first I was amazed how hard I found it to pray without stopping for only five minutes. I thought it would be easy, but it was not. So I made it into a kind of spiritual weight-lifting exercise: *Let's see if I can do five minutes of spiritual "push-ups" and then stretch it a bit further next time.* So, next time you are driving, why not ask the Lord, "How can I use this time—should I pray?"

Walking

Personally I love walking and talking time with God. Prayer walking can really connect you with the geography and community, as we will discuss further in chapter 4. If you want to be able to pray for your neighbors or your city, there is no better way than to get out and walk the streets. People tend to pray differently outside buildings than inside them, so prayer walking is good for bringing a fresh dimension to your prayer life. Maybe you already do this individually, but what about groups of people or the whole church going prayer walking? We tend to have the mentality that corporate prayer takes place only inside. But why don't we take our church outside and have a prayer meeting?

Geographical location

Where you pray can also influence how you pray. You will pray very differently if you are sitting alone on the side of a high mountain with a clear view, compared to sitting in the center of a busy market. Praying by water can also be a wonderful inspiration for prayer; streams and rivers can be very peaceful places to pray. What about praying by the sea—standing and watching the awesome power of the waves? Maybe you do not live too near to the coast or any kind of water, but sometimes it is worth traveling somewhere special just to pray. Think about what would evoke a different kind of prayer in you. Different atmospheres will result in different kinds of prayer.

In the bathtub?

This might raise a smile, but I had a good friend who was powerfully touched by God in the bathtub! My friend really wanted God to fill her with the Holy Spirit so she could begin to speak in tongues, but for some reason she could never get the breakthrough. So I said to her, "Where do you relax the most?" and she replied, "In the bathtub, I suppose." So I gave her this advice: "Next time you are in the house on your own, fill your bathtub up, put loads of bubbles in, relax and just begin to give thanks to God and ask Him to fill you with His Spirit and give you your prayer language." So she planned a time, got in the bathtub and prayed, and God filled her with the Spirit so that she began to speak in her prayer language for the first time. The next time I saw her she was so excited. She rushed up to me and said, "Rachel, it worked! At last I was relaxed. God connected with me and I had the breakthrough. But . . . " she said, "I've had this terrible thought." "What's that?" I asked. "God saw me naked!" she replied earnestly. I could not help but laugh. We sometimes have strange ideas about how God sees us!

Sleeping?

Can you pray when you are asleep? Yes! I have somehow developed the art of communicating with God in my sleep and it is something that irritates my husband, Gordon, terribly!

I believe that my spirit has been connected with the Holy Spirit of God, so even when my physical body is asleep, my spirit can be wide awake. So I have begun to say as I go to sleep each night, "Lord, even as I am asleep, speak to my spirit." As a result, many of my sermons or revelations have been received when I was asleep! God tends to give me headlines or phrases that I remember when I awaken and they start me thinking. They come into my head and I know that the Holy Spirit has dictated them to me in my sleep.

> I will praise the LORD, who counsels me;
> *even at night my heart instructs me.*
>
> Psalm 16:7, emphasis added

So why not experiment with different positions for prayer that will help you to pray differently? Add to those positions an attitude of faith and believe that God will use them for a specific purpose: to build a creative house of prayer for your life.

Types of prayer

Moving on from the positions we can use to express ourselves in prayer, I want to look at the words that describe the different *types* of prayer we can engage in and what they mean. In reality there are hundreds of different ways in which we can communicate in prayer, but I have chosen to focus on just a few key types.

Supplication

Supplication is a prayer that cries out for grace. It has a strong sense of appeal. One Bible commentator has illustrated it in terms of a dog begging for a cookie from his master. Imagine you are eating a chocolate cookie and there is a dog sitting in front of you. The way in which that dog's eyes look at you longingly—that is supplication! Supplication is a heart that is crying out to God just as Habakkuk did:

> LORD . . .
>   in wrath remember mercy.
>
> Habakkuk 3:2

Supplication is a cry that pleads, "God, we are Your people. Don't give us what we deserve, but in these days answer us. Hear our cry. We need Your grace and mercy." Supplicative prayer does not always sound very elegant, as it is a strong, earnest cry from the heart—this is the sound that we hear so often in the Psalms.

Asking or petitioning

Sometimes all that is required of us in prayer is simple asking— an uncomplicated prayer about our needs. In Matthew 7:7 we read the simple command, "Ask and it will be given to you." The Greek verb is constructed in its present-continuous-active form, so in English it very much carries the sense of, "Ask and keep on asking and it will be given and keep on being given to you." This kind of prayer reveals an everyday dependency on God. We need to live with an asking attitude! Because of our tendency to drift into religiosity we can think that we are asking too much of God: "Who are we to keep bothering God with our requests? Isn't it a bit presumptuous?" The answer, of course, is no. It is not presumptuous; it is perfectly normal in the relationship between a child and his or her father. If you have children, then you know that they keep on asking for things! We can ask God for anything—complex or simple. We are not a nuisance to God! He wants to hear our voice. Asking is part of our relationship.

"Asking" in Scripture goes from the micro to the macro. It includes our everyday personal needs, but then God says,

> Ask of Me, and I will give You
> The nations for Your inheritance,
> And the ends of the earth for Your possession.
>
> Psalm 2:8, NKJV

Isn't that incredible? Sometimes people say to me that they find it very hard to intercede for their nation. I tell them, "Don't worry about it. Start by simply 'asking' God for your nation. As you begin to simply ask, God will put that nation in your heart and He will begin to speak to you, revealing things that you can pray for." What began as a simple asking prayer can become a conversation and very soon it has changed into intercession.

Intercession

Intercession is prayer that represents the needs of another person before God. It is prayer that stands in the gap. An *intercessor* is literally one who "fills the gap," one who mediates between two parties.

In Numbers 16:48 we see a lovely description of intercession in the person of Aaron. It says,

> He [Aaron] stood between the living and the dead, and the plague stopped.

Every time you come in intercession you are standing between the living and the dead. Maybe a friend of yours has a "dead" situation financially and God will ask you to stand in the gap and pray on his or her behalf to see the curse of debt broken. Or you may need to stand in the gap for someone who needs healing and releasing from the power of sickness. Intercession is a priestly role in which you come before the Lord to represent someone in need, praying that God will act on his or her behalf because of your cries.

Intercession can be for communities as well as individuals. We need to stand in the gap between the living and the dead for our neighbors, our region and our city. As we increase our time in prayer, I believe God will increase our revelation and give us discernment regarding the spiritual powers that are motivating or affecting people. Armed with such information, we can pray more focused and effective prayers and see previously hopeless situations turned around.

Thanksgiving

Thanksgiving was a type of prayer that the Holy Spirit really had to teach me to pray. I used to think I was a fairly thankful person, but increasingly God has shown me just how much I take for granted and how unthankful I can be. God showed me that, especially in the West, we do not naturally have an attitude of gratitude! Too often we go to God and pray with this kind of attitude: "Oh, Lord, this is wrong and that is wrong. . . . Will You sort it out, please?" We come with a crisis mentality, with the sole agenda of getting our problems solved. Once they are solved we are not very quick to come back into God's presence and say, "Oh, Lord, I so want to thank You for this. . . ."

Have you ever prayed with someone about an issue and later discovered via a third party that the prayer had been answered, but the person concerned never told you? You might even go and ask them, "Why didn't you tell me?" Usually the reply will be, "I forgot!" It makes you wonder, if someone was healed or their baby was conceived, their financial situation turned around, how could they forget to say thank you? But we all do it, regularly. Often in our Western culture we have an attitude of, "You owe this to me," and so this does not encourage an atmosphere of thanksgiving. We often forget that we have prayed and miss the fact that *we do have* a God who answers prayer, but by doing so we lose the incredible sense of joy and celebration that our Daddy in heaven heard our prayers and answered them.

We need to ask God to cultivate our attitude of gratitude. In many of the epistles whenever Paul summarizes his final instructions to the believers, you will find somewhere in his list "thanksgiving." I've selected just one of these Scriptures in Philippians:

> Rejoice in the Lord always. I will say it again: Rejoice! Let your gentleness be evident to all. The Lord is near. Do not be anxious about anything, but in *everything, by prayer and petition, with thanksgiving,* present your requests to God.
>
> Philippians 4:4–6, emphasis added

What a perfect mix: Thanksgiving blended with requests.

An attitude of thanksgiving is an attractive atmosphere that is like a magnet to the presence of God. In Psalm 100:4 it says, "Enter his gates with thanksgiving."

Aren't we always more willing to listen to a person who comes to us in a thankful attitude? If you sense someone is coming to see you so that he or she can moan and whine, aren't you much less likely to want to listen and help them?

I once had one of those wonderful days that rarely happen as a mother, where the house was clean, meals for the day were planned and I had achieved all I wanted to do that day. I was clock-watching, thinking, *The kids will be home soon.* Sure enough I heard the back gate, footsteps along the path and then the back door was thrown open. But the first words my son shouted were, "Mom, where's my football gear? Why isn't it clean?" and all my expectation and longing to have them home evaporated as I felt that I had failed. I had looked forward to everyone arriving back home, hoping that they would notice my work in the home and be grateful. But, as I heard their demands as the door flew open, I heard the Holy Spirit speak to me: *Rachel, I wait in eager expectation for your footsteps. I wait to hear you come and enter My presence. I wait for that door of fellowship to open so I can listen to your voice. But so often as you throw open the door what I hear is, "God! What are You doing?" You enter My presence with the strong sound of complaining.* Needless to say, this challenged me and I realized how my own attitude needed adjusting. We need to enter God's presence with thanksgiving in our mouths!

Confession

An important and vital aspect of our prayer life must be the simple discipline of prayers of confession. We often tend to wait too long before approaching God when we know we have done something wrong. We would lead much happier and more peaceful lives if we learned to come before our Father and say, "Dear Lord, I am sorry. I've sinned." How many of us have sinned since the day we got saved? All of us, I am sure! So where did we get this strange idea that the prayer of confession is something that only Catholics should do? I believe every Christian needs times of confessional prayer before God. We need to regularly come before the cross and say, "I'm sorry, Lord, I have sinned. I really blew it!"

If we deal with our sin swiftly and honestly, we are also dealing with the roots of our guilt, our shame and our sense of failure. Too many people walk around stooped over with guilt and condemnation, feeling like second-class Christians. But if you go to God, confess your sin and repent, then you can walk with the assurance that Jesus' blood has washed your sins away. Then you can enter the place of intimacy with God and enjoy

His presence without feeling guilty. You stand righteous, clean and redeemed because you have handed over your sin to Jesus. Many people do not readily pray the prayer of confession because they see it as the prayer of failure. No, it is not like that; rather, it is the prayer of release!

First John 1:9 says,

> If we confess our sins, he is faithful and just and will forgive us our sins and purify us from all unrighteousness.

Notice the verse says "if"! We have got to do something if we want to receive the bonus of the promise. My husband, Gordon, always says, "God forgives the guilty, not the pathetic." So often we come into God's presence acting pathetic with reasons and excuses why we have sinned, blaming circumstances or other people. Instead, we need to take responsibility for our choices and decisions and own our sin, confess it, and God will purify us.

So as part of building your house of prayer, you need to build a confessional room, a place that you visit regularly to say you are sorry.

Forgiveness

I believe that the partnership of the prayer of confession with the prayer of forgiveness is a powerful combination. Most parents will tell you that it is difficult to train your child to say: "I'm sorry" and "I forgive you." The sad thing is, we are not much different in the Church. We still find it really hard to apologize and take responsibility for wrong attitudes that we have toward each other and then to forgive, so we need to ask God to help us to be generous with our forgiveness.

We need to look at this area of prayer both in the individual and corporate dimensions. When was the last time at your church you had an evening devoted to confessing sins, to apologizing and forgiving one another? When was the last time you had a service based on the theme of forgiveness? Of course you must forgive as an individual, but think how God could use this prayer corporately. I believe that if churches prayed prayers of forgiveness together regularly, it would heal the pain of offense that so many people carry.

People often leave their churches as they get offended with one another. When this happens, the issue is rarely dealt with, so division and conflict wound the Church once again. But if we would only learn how to forgive and release one another, it would save so much heartbreak and many church splits. We need to settle our accounts swiftly.

The prayer of forgiveness is a generous prayer that costs you something. Not everyone who hurts you in life will come to you and apologize. Some people are totally unaware that they have even hurt you, but nevertheless you must forgive them. Just as Jesus cried out from the cross, "Father, forgive them. They don't know what they are doing," so we must learn to forgive others regardless of their attitude toward us. Sometimes you can be hurt by well-meaning people who honestly do not realize they are wounding you. They will probably never come to the revelation of what they are doing to you, so you have to make a choice to forgive them anyway. Even though they will never understand how hurtful their behavior was, you still have to pray the prayer of forgiveness and let go of all offense. Remember, it is your life that depends on this—you need to pray this prayer to live!

Prayer of proclamation

This prayer has a strong authoritative sound. It speaks and declares. We see this in Jesus' life when He came across a boy who was demon possessed. Jesus prayed a simple prayer of proclamation: "Be delivered." When Jesus met the blind man who wanted to see, He commanded the blind eyes to "Be opened!" and they were. When Jesus stood up in the disciples' boat while they were still in the midst of the storm, He prayed and simply declared, "Peace. Be still."

This is a completely different type of prayer from supplication or intercession, but one which I believe God wants us to move into in these days. We can pray prayers of proclamation as the Holy Spirit reveals the situation to us and then gives us language to declare it out loud.

Several years ago I was in a ladies' conference in Norway when a lady named Margaret Froen was brought into the back of the meeting. Someone came to the front and grabbed me and took me to this lady, saying, "Please, come and pray for her." I looked at her and vaguely recognized her, and then realized she was the wife of one of the YWAM people in Norway. She was desperately sick—in fact, so ill that I could hardly believe it was her.

She was lying on a couch and could not lift up her head. She looked so frail and it seemed inappropriate to pray with her in any other tone than very gently and quietly, but before I could stop myself, a loud cry of proclamation rose up in me and I yelled at the top of my voice, "No! You will not die!" It was such an aggressive prayer that I was totally taken aback by it, but I knew deep down that God had prompted it. The Holy Spirit then touched her dramatically and she began to shake. After I had prayed over her, I needed to visit the bathroom and when I came back she had gone. I cringed and thought perhaps I had really offended her.

Around two weeks later the phone rang at home and it was Margaret. She had been totally healed. Today she is still alive and in ministry alongside her husband in Norway. God did a work through that prayer of proclamation. It may not always sound nice, but I believe that God stirs this shout of proclamation and it should have a place in our prayer lifestyle.

Silence or waiting

Our prayer does not have to be limited to spoken words. Communication is so much more than just words. How many of us remember that look in our mother's eye across the table when there were visitors for dinner? There was a lot of communication flowing in the glance but not a word was spoken, and you knew that if you moved another inch you were in for it!

We can communicate powerfully with God through silence. You can try it right now by using this simple technique: Think of a particular attribute of God—His love, His majesty or His faithfulness—and then focus on that attribute, silently giving thanks for that aspect of His character. As you do this, prayer will rise to the throne of God, though not a word will be spoken. If you continue to sit silently for a time before God, focusing on Him in this way, eventually the sweetness of His presence will come to you. It is in that still and silent place that you touch the heart of God. There are times to shout and declare but there are times to whisper. In the place of silent intimacy, a sudden prayer of proclamation would be totally inappropriate; the silent communication of the heart is all that is needed. An incredible range of information can be exchanged between you and the Lord that goes beyond words as deep calls to deep.

Have you ever been really weary, so tired that you feel you can't even find the strength to pray? In those times you can come and just lie in God's presence, saying, "Lord, I'm beyond words. I haven't got any words to offer. But everything in me is calling out to You. I need You."

These silent times become an important part of your prayer life as you discover it is in these times God can speak and give you strategies. When you are still, it allows God the opportunity to share His heart with you. We tend to rush into God's presence armed with requests and many burdens, and we think that we have finished praying and are ready to head out the door once we have released these to God, and so we miss our opportunity to hear the Holy Spirit saying, "No, wait!" because now it is God's time to talk to you.

Whenever you pray you should always expect God to speak back to you. So much of hearing God has nothing to do with dramatic voices booming from the heavens; it is about learning God's gentle nudges, the instincts of the Spirit. God's voice can be as subtle as a thought. When it comes you know it wasn't your thought, but a God-thought.

When Gordon and I were pastoring, several times God saved us from disasters by speaking a quiet word into our hearts during times of silent waiting on Him. I remember one particular morning on our day off when I just kept thinking about a particular lady in our church. In the end I said, "Gordon, I really feel that we need to go and buy her some flowers and stop by and see her quickly before we go out for the day." So we did and when we arrived she said to us, "Oh, I wondered if you would remember." I was frantically thinking, *Oh no, what are we meant to be remembering? God help me!* The flowers turned out to be appropriate as she continued, saying, "It was a year ago today that my husband died." I thought, *Thank You, Father, for directing us.* I had not remembered but the Holy Spirit had. I was able to say to this lady, "To tell you the truth, I didn't remember, but the Holy Spirit did and He told me I was to come and bring you flowers today."

Praying in the Spirit

Jude 1:20 says, "Build yourselves up in your most holy faith and pray in the Holy Spirit."

Most people either seem to be very good at praying in the Spirit or very bad—there are not too many in between. There are a few churches where I go to lead prayer where, when I call upon people to pray, all you can hear is people praying in their heavenly prayer language. I think it is important to have a balanced prayer voice—we need to pray both with our understanding and to pray in the Spirit.

One of the pitfalls in building your house of prayer is that you often get stuck in a rut whereby you always enter by the same door. You probably have several entrances to your natural home: a front door, a back or side door, maybe a patio door. Most of us get into the routine of entering by the same door whenever we return home. We can be like that in our prayer lives, too. We get into a habit of entering our personal house of prayer by using the same door every time. In other words, we always use the same style, the same approach. Well, use a different door! Because every time you enter your house of prayer through a different door, it will feel fresh and different. Try to balance things by using other methods of prayer. If you like to pray in tongues a lot, balance it with prayers in English. When you pray in tongues you don't always know what you are praying for, so it is a good discipline to pray with your understanding, too.

Praying in the Spirit is like giving your "spiritual man" vitamin tonic! In 1 Corinthians 14:4 it says that a person who speaks in tongues edifies himself. If you look at the root of that word *edify*, it literally means "to grow, to enlarge, to increase, to give capacity to." So if you feel like your spirit is unnourished and the size of a skinny stick insect and you need more spiritual muscle, then increase your praying in the Spirit! The Holy Spirit will grow and enlarge your spiritual capacity and enlarge your ability and effectiveness. Your spirit-man will grow and, like a vitamin tonic, praying in the Spirit will strengthen your stamina and ability to pray.

Fasting

Why do fasting and prayer go together? I believe it is because prayer is so much more than words. God uses attitudes to come alongside prayer to expand our prayer life. Fasting is so complementary to prayer because both these acts involve sacrifice, and it is the attitude of sacrifice that creates an atmosphere that attracts the heart of God. In fasting, God is asking us to exchange our natural appetite for our spiritual appetite. Fasting is simply us saying to God, "I want You more than I want my food!"

Sometimes God challenges us to fast from things other than our food. Maybe it would be good for you to specifically fast from chocolate for a while, or from playing a sport, or from watching TV. A young man who was consumed with a passion to play football once said to me, "I think the Holy Spirit has told me to fast from football for a while. Do you think that sounds like God?" I said, "Yes, if that is your addictive appetite."

Fasting is giving something up for a season as a specific offering to God and then connecting that sacrifice to definite times of prayer. It is this connection that is important. That's why the Bible says, "Fast and pray." Some people tend to "fast and play"! They do not do much praying, they just fast for a bit! Or, alternatively, they may "feast and pray"! But when we connect fasting and praying together, something dynamic happens. It moves our prayers beyond words.

In Matthew 6:16–17 we see the small phrase *"when* you fast . . ."* (emphasis added). It is a "when" rather than an "if," which means the Bible is *expecting* you to fast occasionally. It is not an optional extra for the superstar Christian. Apart from valid medical reasons, we should expect fasting to be part of our prayer life for short seasons.

Written prayer

If you are anything like me, then I am sure you really appreciate reading the psalms. They exist because the psalmists took the time to write down their prayers. Some regard written prayers, like Anglican liturgy, as belonging to an "old style" of church and say, "Thank goodness we don't need those anymore!" On the contrary, I believe there is incredible power in written prayer.

On a corporate level, it is very helpful for a church to have a prayerfully crafted mission statement. It gives the church a continual reminder of its focus and purpose. If intercessory groups write a prayer of declaration that the leadership agrees to, it can be a very powerful tool for unified prayer. Whenever God's people come together with one voice, one heart, one mind, focused on a specific goal or vision, powerful results will be achieved.

Remember the Table for Two? There is something very beautiful and powerful about writing a prayer to God that is like a love letter. I love it when Gordon writes me a letter or a poem. We almost have a tradition now, poor man, that for every birthday, Christmas, or any other special occasion, I expect to receive a poem from him! There is something very beautiful about a person expressing himself or herself to you in writing. Take time out on your prayer journey to do this and write a letter to God expressing your heart. Written words have power.

Creative arts and prayer

What about painted prayers or danced prayers? No, I have not gone mad! I believe this is a time in the Church when there will be an increasing release of artistic creativity. We have limited prayer to merely speaking communication, but the younger generations are much more visual and multimedia oriented. If you go into a young person's bedroom, it is not uncommon for him or her to be talking with their friend on the phone, have music playing in the background, and maybe have the TV on as well, and all the time have the computer on while attempting to do homework! "Are you working?" the parent asks. "Yes!" the incredulous teenager replies. "What's your problem?" Time in the house of prayer, therefore, can be much more interactive than we have made it, especially if we want to engage our young people. We have got to let that creativity come into the house!

Figuratively speaking, you might want to paint your own personal house of prayer your favorite color, but the corporate house of prayer will need to be many different colors. There will be some colors present that you may not like that much, but they are accepted by God just as much as yours are. It is a bit like when your kids want to decorate their own bedrooms. You may be horrified by their choice of color scheme or decor, but it would be wrong to stifle and suppress their creative expression; just guide it a little! Similarly in the house of prayer, you have to let each person decorate his or her room—even if it does not look like your perfect room.

I have watched numbers of people actually paint pictures during times of worship and create an incredible expression of their heart toward God, which has been powerful and has communicated something deep. I have also watched people dance and that has communicated something very powerful, too. We need to let this creative prayer out.

Sung prayer

A number of musicians have said to me they find it hard to pray. I usually respond by saying, "The problem is you are trying to use the wrong language! You are a musician and your communication language is notes and keys, not words. When you want to pray, pick up your guitar and start to strum, or sit at your keyboard and start to play and you will soon be praying. When you play, you bring an atmosphere of prayer and you trigger your spirit to talk. You say you can't find the right words, yet every time you sit at the keyboard, I hear a prayer!"

I believe it is possible to talk to God through music. For musicians especially, I believe that this is an essential part of their prayer life.

Sometimes when I find I have no fluency of expression with spoken words when praying, I will begin to sing. Often I will put on a worship CD and begin to sing and, for me at least, the music triggers words of prayer. Different people will have different triggers. Some of us are stimulated by what we see, by vibrant colors, so watching a painting take shape as described previously will trigger prayer for you while for others it is the sound of music.

What are your triggers? What are the atmospheres that make you come alive? Put those things into your house of prayer.

Aids to prayer

There are many aids to prayer I could discuss, but here I have listed just a few suggestions you might want to consider:

- Banners with topics
- Missions' newsletters/bulletins
- Maps of your local area
- A globe or flags of the nations
- Photographs of family members
- Testimonies
- Going prayer walking in your neighborhood
- Forming prayer triplets with a focused project
- A prayer scrapbook with collection information
- Statistics/newspaper articles
- Prayer requests

These are all tools that can stimulate a broader dimension of prayer. Find out what works for you so that you are able to build your house of prayer. Ask God to breathe new creativity into your prayer life.

Let us pray:

Father, today I ask You again—teach me to pray! I want to learn how to communicate with You in my personal and individual language style. Father, I am asking You to stretch my vocabulary and my experience of prayer. Let me learn to enjoy my house of prayer and to create a vibrant atmosphere of love and passion for You in this place of prayer. Amen.

Being Prepared as a Vessel for Prayer

As you ask God to teach you to pray, He will put His hand on your life and prepare you as a vessel for prayer. This is an exciting journey of discovery! But so often people shrink back feeling that perhaps prayer is not "their thing." That is never true. If you feel this way it just means you need God's hand to come upon you and guide you. There is a world of difference between the passion that has a *desperate desire* to pray, and the feeling of *the crushing duty* that you ought to pray. Allow yourself to be touched by God and let Him form you into a vessel for prayer. I hope the following story from my own testimony will illustrate what I mean.

In 1984 my husband, Gordon, and I had just arrived in Zimbabwe to work alongside evangelist Reinhard Bonnke in his Christ for All Nations ministry. I was 24 years old at the time and was naively determined that we were going to be "the men and women of power for the hour," here to change the nation. I went with an attitude of "Watch out, Zimbabwe, here we come!" But just six weeks later I was involved in a serious traffic accident and was fighting for my life.

It was October 27, 1984, and we had been conducting a crusade in Harare. About 25,000 people had attended the meeting on this particular evening and we had seen God working in miraculous ways. Leaving the meeting, we had just arrived home when we heard the sound of a serious car accident right outside our house. We arrived at the scene and discovered that several ministers of President Mugabe's government had been injured in the accident. Immediately we got involved and began administering first aid to the injured. But while I was busy attending to the crushed people inside the car, a seven-ton military truck came down the hill toward the traffic lights outside our home and plowed into the stationary vehicles. Suddenly I realized what was happening, but it was too late to escape, and I was crushed between this truck and the cars.

Everything from my hips down was crushed in the impact and both my legs were broken in many different places. Having stopped to help people injured in a car crash, I now found myself in an ambulance, being rushed to a hospital in Harare. I remember thinking, *God, I came here to change the world and now this has happened. What is going on?*

Initially it seemed that my fractured bones were my main problem. Once my legs were set in plaster, I was told it would take three to four months to heal and I would be confined to a wheelchair for awhile. At the time, my daughter Nicola was just six months old and I wondered how on earth I was going to cope looking after her while in my wheelchair. But just twelve hours later a serious complication set in. Sometimes when a bone is broken, fat tissue can seep into the bloodstream, causing a fat embolism. This fat then travels through the bloodstream through the lungs, heart and up into the brain stem, causing a life-threatening condition. Unfortunately, I began to have multiple fat emboli and slipped into a coma. As I fell into this deep coma, the medical staff was increasingly concerned by my lack of response after three days. Then a scan revealed that there was extensive brain damage and so they expected me to die shortly. Word was sent to my family to come to my bedside to say good-bye.

This may sound strange, but I am grateful in so many ways that such a terrible accident happened to me in Zimbabwe and not in England, my home nation. Any English person would no doubt think they would be better off in England where there is better *medical care*. But no, I was happy it happened in Africa where they have better *miracle care*! In Africa the people are not afraid to passionately get hold of God for hours and pray with a strong authority: "No! Rachel will not die. She will live." And that is exactly what they did. Despite the fact that I had only been in Africa for six short weeks and they hardly knew me, I later discovered that five churches across Harare joined together to storm heaven night and day until God restored me to health. Twenty-four hours a day there were never less than a thousand people praying for God to do a miracle!

As quickly as they were able, my parents arrived in Harare and rushed to my bedside. My dad, being a man of great faith, stood at the end of my bed and read out the following declaration based on Psalm 118:17–18:

> Rachel, you shall not die but live for the Lord, and you will proclaim that which is within you. For God has chastened you severely, but has not given you over to death.

Somehow that was a turning point for my life, because five hours later I woke up totally *compos mentis*. God had healed me. I still had two broken legs, but He had healed me from the life-threatening emboli and restored my brain to normal function instantly (although my kids still doubt this sometimes!).

That was the start of a journey that lasted several years until finally my entire body was fully restored and healed. I spent the ensuing eight months in a wheelchair while my bones knit back together. After that, walking was very painful for a long time. As soon as I was able to stand, Gordon and I made the decision to return to work alongside Reinhard Bonnke, first in Africa and then in the Philippines. It was there, almost four years after my accident, that a couple named Charles and Frances Hunter prayed over me and God touched me powerfully.

The Hunters were visiting the Philippines and we were invited to one of their meetings. Charles, whom I did not know at that time, came over to me and asked me outright, "Excuse me, but can I ask you—is there anything wrong with your body due to a traffic accident?" A little shocked, I said, "Well, yes, there is." Immediately he said he would like to pray for me and as he did so, he reached down and touched my leg. I did not feel anything at the time, but he then said to me, "Now, do something you could not do before I prayed for you."

Ever since the accident I had not been able to walk anywhere easily without wearing shoes because my right leg was twisted and much shorter than my left. I simply could not get my right heel to touch the ground. Apprehensively I took my left shoe off first and then my right and found that for the first time since the accident, both my heels touched the ground. I knew at that moment that God had miraculously lengthened and straightened my right leg. The pain subsided and I have been able to walk perfectly ever since that time.

God had done so much for me, so naturally I had an immense sense of gratitude in my heart. I could not help but be overwhelmed with a sense of "Wow! People have prayed. I should have died but I am alive. God has healed me!" When you have had a near-death experience and know God answered prayer, trust me, you do believe in prayer like never before! But I also discovered that even though I had such an incredible encounter with God—such an experience of the healing power that came through persevering prayer—I still found it difficult to have a disciplined personal prayer life.

I wanted to be a mighty intercessor for nations! But I remember I would sit in my wheelchair and decide to pray for Zimbabwe and after about five minutes I would run out of prayers. I began to think, *God, what is the matter with me? I want to pray. I'm totally convinced of the power of prayer. So why can't I pray?*

One day when I cried out to God in frustration, He clearly spoke to me with the answer: "Rachel," He said, "stop *trying* so hard to pray. First let Me touch your heart and teach you to love."

I realized immediately what I had been doing. So often in our walk with God we try to find the capacity within ourselves to do what we know we ought to do. We try to summon up the strength and desire to accomplish things for God, when He is waiting to supply us with His supernatural power.

Good prayer depends on the condition of your heart. We will never succeed in interceding for others unless God has touched our heart with compassion for those people. God has to touch your heart and teach you to understand the cry of those you pray for: the pain of divorce, the emptiness of drug abuse, the devastation of alcohol abuse. When you feel what others are feeling, it does something to your heart; it makes you willing to go to the place of prayer, and sacrifice as you pour out your heart to God until something changes.

So my wheelchair became my training school, and I learned that even though I had the most incredible encounter with a prayer-answering God, even that was not enough to keep me in the place of prayer. For the remainder of this chapter, I want to look at the areas of our lives where God wants to touch each one of us if we are to be shaped into a vessel of prayer that He can really use. Here I will share my own personal journey of how God has had to deal with me, but I believe that these are general principles that you will be able to apply to your own life. Remember, prayer often changes you first and then your circumstances!

The five central characteristics of a prayer warrior

1. Love

In every prayer warrior, God seeks to develop the characteristic of agape love. He has to teach us to love like He loves. Why? Because essentially we humans are selfish! In fact, the closer you get to God the more you realize the depth of your selfishness. But prayer is essentially about *sacrifice*. It is more about giving away than it is about receiving. Effective prayer is motivated by unselfish love. Usually we find it really tough to love people when they are difficult, or unknown, or when they are against us—it is not natural for us to love them. That is why your love, and hence your prayers for others, has to come from a divine source. The agape love of God stretches us far beyond our personality.

God's love is something that you receive by faith and is quite separate from the emotional feelings most people associate with the word *love*. You receive it in the same way that you receive other spiritual gifts—by opening yourself up to the Holy Spirit and receiving it by faith. It means you can give the gift of God's love in the same way you would use any other gift from Him—by an act of your will. In other words you can choose to love a person, whether you feel like it or not. You can also extend this love toward groups of people—your community, your city, even your nation. Is it really possible to love a nation so much that you are stirred to pour out your heart to God for it? With the Holy Spirit's help, yes, it is. This is not a natural ability, but a spiritual gift.

It was this deep love that kept Jesus on the cross for you. You must know that no nails could hold Him there against His will. Rather, it was His sense of commission and destiny and His love for the world. *"For God so loved the world."* It was that love that caused Him to endure the cross. And it is this revelation of that overflowing love, and only that love, that will keep you on your knees for other people. There will be many times when you have other things you would rather do, that even seem more important to you, but it is the heartcry of God for people that will motivate you to the place of intercession.

All love has a price tag; it will cost you something. It costs you to give yourself in marriage; it costs you to be a parent. Every father will tell you that love costs—especially if he has daughters! Love cost Jesus His life. The agape love of God is going to cost you yours. God's love brings you to a place where you are willing to lay down your life, where suddenly your priorities are aligned with His priorities. Why? Because the agape love of God takes you to a higher agenda. God's love is going to move you out of your comfort zone.

So often we have a wrong understanding of the grace to pray, and think that intercession flows out of our personality. We think, *She is an intercessor because she's that kind of compassionate person.* I do not believe that your ability as an intercessor is dependent on your personality at all. Intercession flows out of *connectedness* with the Father and is a ministry of love from His heart, through your heart to others. Some people's personalities are naturally more merciful and more compassionate than others, but if the source and basis for their intercession is their own personality, before long they will burn out.

I have met many tired intercessors who have ministered in the place of prayer out of their personality rather than from a divinely motivated love. If you do that, then you will get tired. All of us, regardless of our personality, need to be connected to

God's love. So how do we let this love develop in our hearts? I believe the following three steps are important:

▶ *Make a decision not to act out of your emotional response, but respond to the instruction of God*
You need to ask God to show you the areas where He wants you to pray and then, by faith, receive His love and His ability to touch that area. Ask God to give you your spiritual prayer assignments for this season of your life. Never allow yourself to be driven by your feelings of guilt or pity alone. Bring your emotions to God and then ask Him to show you what is your responsibility in the particular situation.

▶ *Be forgiving*
If you really want to know and feel the love of God, then you need to be a generous forgiver. Forgiveness is not a selective emotion. If you have an issue with another person and refuse to forgive him or her, then you are surrounding yourself with an atmosphere of unforgiveness. You cannot harbor unforgiveness against one person and yet show incredible love toward another. An unforgiving person tends to become more and more isolated as her or she refuses to deal with the root issue. You have to deal with your unforgiveness before you can truly receive and give away love. Then, in that place of being able to receive the unconditional love of God, you can begin to pray.

▶ *Deal with the terror of fear*
Fear is a major stronghold in many of our lives. When we are fearful, we find it difficult to pray effectively as we cannot trust the face of God to hear and answer us. The apostle John wrote about the conflict between love and fear and taught that we need a revelation of God's love in our lives so that we can drive out the fear that controls us (see 1 John 4:16–19). Fear needs to

be dealt with ruthlessly. If fear is occupying an area of your heart, then guess what? God's love can't be present in that area. Love and fear are opposites.

If you have areas of fear in your life, then you need a specific revelation of the vastness of God's love for you in that particular area. If you are worried about money, for example, then you need a revelation of the truth that your Father in heaven is your provider. When you have a revelation that your Daddy in heaven provides for you, then the power of fear over your finances is broken.

Focusing on the roots, not the fruit

Often we concentrate on the fruit or evidence of love and ask God, "Lord, make me more loving." We want more love demonstrated through our lives. Immediately we think of Galatians 5:22: "The fruit of the Spirit is love, joy, peace...." But I want us to also remember Ephesians 3:16–17, which speaks of being *rooted* in love. Most gardeners will tell you that if you have poor fruit, it is because you have poor roots. If you want to have great fruit, then you need to invest something in the soil. It is the same with love. If you want to demonstrate the love of God to others, then you have to be deeply rooted in a revelation of this love. Paul wrote,

> I pray that out of his glorious riches he may strengthen you with power through his Spirit in your inner being, so that Christ may dwell in your hearts through faith. And I pray *that you, being rooted and established in love...*
>
> Ephesians 3:16–17, emphasis added

If you are rooted in God's love, then guess what is going to be the fruit? His love. Get securely rooted. Prayer is the place of communication where God will really begin to speak to you and reveal to you how much He loves you. Once you are truly rooted in His love, without any great effort you will find that His love begins to bear fruit. After this encounter you discover a new grace on your life, which enables you to love the unlovely, love the objectionable, love those who speak against you, because God's love is in you.

Prayer changes you, and as you commit your life to prayer, your prayer will change your love capacity!

2. Compassion

The second quality that God wants to develop in our lives as we learn to pray is compassion. In 1990 God gave me a vision of the type of army He is building—an army of compassionate prayer warriors. In the vision I saw an army of ordinary people made up from many nations. There were men and women of all ages and from different backgrounds—some were rich business executives, others were poor and needy. There were Americans, Africans, Asians, Europeans—all sorts of people—and they were marching. The amazing thing was—they were marching on their knees! And as they marched they were crying out to God and tears ran down their cheeks. Then God spoke to me and said, "Rachel, the army that marches with true victory will be the army that marches on its knees with hearts overflowing with compassion."

The Lord told me that the kneeling symbolized *prayer, humility* and *servanthood,* and that the tears represented *compassion.* So often we think that we must become a vast and aggressive prayer army in order to impact nations spiritually, but actually I believe it will be an army on its knees that will do the most damage to the enemy's kingdom.

If the agape love of God is working in your heart, then compassion is the outward expression of that love through your body and soul. Compassion is love translated to the hands.

People instinctively know the difference between pity and genuine compassion. I remember it well from my time in the wheelchair. True compassion comes from within as God does a work in you, enabling you to reach out to others. It is what filled Jesus when He saw so many people sinking in a sea of hopelessness.

> When he [Jesus] saw the crowds, he had compassion on them, because they were harassed and helpless, like sheep without a shepherd. Then he said to his disciples, "The harvest is plentiful but the workers are few. Ask the Lord of the harvest, therefore, to send out workers into his harvest field."
>
> Matthew 9:36–38

I noticed something about these verses a while ago: We are always asking God to send us a great harvest, and yet God's cry is different. He is saying, "Send Me the workers—the harvest is ready and waiting!"

What prevents us from going into the harvest field then? We are simply unaware of the harvest; we have grown so familiar with the people around us that we can no longer see them. We ask God for a harvest and God says, "It's right there in front of you!" But once our eyes of compassion are opened, suddenly we are aware of a vast harvest of souls "helpless, like sheep without a shepherd," waiting for someone to guide them into the truth.

Compassion literally means to "suffer alongside others." It carries a sense of empathy that does not look down on others in pity, but rather comes alongside, puts an arm around them and feels their distress. *Compassion* also means, "to be moved inwardly; to be affected similarly; to show mercy or kindness; to give assistance; to bear with; to be touched emotionally." Compassion cannot work from a distance; it needs to be close and connected. Jesus saw the complete picture of the state of the people of His community and it moved Him; it touched Him; it provoked Him to want to do something about it.

I have found that God has had to work on my heart to fill me with compassion. My natural background is a research scientist. I studied biochemistry in college and worked as a clinical biochemist in the area of hormone research for several years before going into full-time ministry. Naturally I have a logical mind that enjoys administration and process more than the touchy-feely world of people and their problems. Consequently, I was a very rational, "just get on with it" type of person. In fact, the wheelchair was a good learning experience for me, because I had always been a very capable, independent person, and suddenly I needed help in simple, everyday things. So God has had to teach me something: Without compassion I am a danger to others! He had to show me that people are more precious than paper or systems and that compassion is essential for good prayer warriors.

This is something that we all need to learn. Your journey will be different from mine, but the outcome will be the same. God wants to teach us to love others and to be compassionate. Compassionate people are people who can be trusted with the secrets of those who are hurting.

The following three Scriptures illustrate the three stages God will take you through to develop a compassionate heart:

▶ *Ezekiel 11:19:*

> "I will give them an undivided heart and put a new spirit in them; I will remove from them their heart of stone and give them a heart of flesh."

God wants to remove our stony hearts and give us hearts of flesh. We need some heart surgery so that every area of hardness is removed! God wants to correct the way in which we react to certain types of people, to remove the stones of prejudice, cultural barriers, economic barriers, offense and woundedness. God wants our heart to be soft again so that it can respond quickly to anyone in need. The heart of flesh will feel pain, when the stony heart feels nothing!

▶ *Isaiah 57:15:*

> For this is what the high and lofty One says—
>   he who lives forever, whose name is holy:
> "I live in a high and holy place,
>   but also with him who is contrite and lowly in spirit,
> to revive the spirit of the lowly
>   and to revive the heart of the contrite."

If God is going to give you a compassionate heart, then He has to remove all pride—especially the sense that looks down on others, rather than releasing love unconditionally. There is nothing worse than reluctant compassion given from a height at a great price! It has to be brought down low and come alongside a person. This Scripture tells us that God is comfortable to mix among the humble. We need to be people that God is happy to work with. If there is any arrogance in our hearts, then we will never be true co-workers with God, expressing authentic compassion.

▶ *Revelation 3:16–18:*

> "So, because you are lukewarm—neither hot nor cold—I am about to spit you out of my mouth. You say, 'I am rich; I have acquired wealth and do not need a thing.' But you do not realize that you are wretched, pitiful, poor, blind and naked. I counsel you to buy from me gold refined in the fire, so you

can become rich; and white clothes to wear, so you can cover your shameful nakedness; and salve to put on your eyes, so you can see."

Finally, God needs to remove all biased attitudes and every area of blindness from our lives if we are to be consistently compassionate. This Scripture in Revelation 3 speaks about the type of person who is pretty confident that he or she has life sorted out: "I'm rich. . . . I don't need anything!" But God responds, "No! You don't realize you are blind. Come to Me and I will anoint your eyes so that you can see." Sometimes we look at our lives and think we are doing okay, but God looks at our hearts and has a different assessment. He wants to touch our eyes so that we are no longer spiritually blind; He wants us to see people as He sees them.

Once I was shopping in a supermarket when I noticed a woman with three kids who were running around behind her and generally causing chaos. One of the children, about six years old, was being fairly disruptive and disobedient but his mother responded by swearing so badly at this child that it shocked me. Each time her son would misbehave she would launch into another tirade of verbal abuse against him; it was like a machine gun going off. After this had happened several times I could not just stand there any longer.

"Sweetie," I said to her, "please be gentle with him." Immediately she rounded on me, eyes glaring, but I just touched her hand lightly and said, "Look, please, I do not mean that as a criticism. I'm a mother of two and I remember the days when my kids drove me to distraction when I went shopping. I suffered for many years with anger. I'm not criticizing you, I just wanted to try and show you a better way." As she looked into my eyes and saw genuine compassion, not correction, her eyes filled with tears and she began to cry. I said to her, "Could I pray for you that God would give you grace to be a mother of three? I know it's not easy and this might sound strange to you, but I believe that God is going to give you positive words to build up your son so that he will grow up to be a son you are proud of." She stood there and let me pray with her and then smiled at me and said, "Thank you so much. I know I need help!" True compassion will always break through.

3. Mercy

Mercy and compassion are closely linked. In the previous illustration you can see that mercy has to come alongside compassion. Mercy is a cry that says, "Oh, God, please don't give them what they deserve." Mercy is a decision to show lenience when you have the power to bring judgment. For instance, imagine you have an appointment but you are late so you end up driving well over the speed limit. Unfortunately, a police officer spots you and in due course you are pulled over. The officer gets his little book out and says to you, "Excuse me, sir/madam, you were breaking the speed limit," and he begins writing the ticket. What do you feel at that point? *Oh, he's right. I deserve this.* But how would you feel if the officer then took the ticket and said, "Don't worry. This time I'm going to pay it for you"? The relief of mercy! You know full well you deserved to pay the penalty, but you have been let off. Mercy is a wonderful thing. All of us need to give mercy to others.

Religion is more concerned with judgment than mercy, because religion is about keeping rules. If you break the rules, then you will certainly pay the price. Often we are guilty of being too religious in our prayers for others because actually, we want them to have to pay the price for their misdemeanors! But God wants to influence the language of our prayer life and make it merciful. We should never pray for people in a "God, you know what they've done" kind of way. Rather, we should pray that they would receive mercy from God, just as He has been merciful to us. God does not treat us with a critical attitude—He is generous toward us—and we need to be generous when we pray for others.

During the recent moves of God across the world, this phrase has become familiar: *God loves you just the way you are . . . but He loves you too much to leave you the way you are!* Our prayers for others should reflect this attitude—completely affirming the person, but calling for the mercy of God to take him or her and restore him or her. This was a response that God has had to teach me. Over the years I have prayed with drug addicts, homosexuals and many broken people. I know from experience that it is possible to find yourself praying that God will touch and bless someone, but secretly be struggling with critical thoughts like *They are only reaping what they've sown.* But would you like to reap what you have sown? I certainly would not! So then we must not let our prayers be contaminated with a judgmental or critical attitude, but overflow with mercy.

Many of us would be like Jonah if God left our attitudes unchallenged. Still today some prophetic people would like to see a bit of judgment to endorse their words as a sign they were from God. Yet these words are given so that people will have time to correct issues in their lives and come to repentance. If the people do turn and repent and then God is able to pour out mercy instead of judgment, then we have done our job!

James 2:13 says, "Mercy triumphs over judgment!" Therefore, you need to ask God to remove every judgmental or critical attitude in your heart on the journey to becoming a reliable vessel for prayer.

4. Identification

Identification is the practical expression of our compassion that positions us to pray alongside the person in his or her pain and circumstances. We know that Jesus literally identified with us. Hebrews 4:15 says of Him,

> For we do not have a high priest who is unable to sympathize with our weaknesses, but we have one who has been tempted in every way, just as we are—yet was without sin.

The total identification of Jesus with us is also movingly described in Isaiah 53:

> Surely he took up our infirmities
>   and carried our sorrows,
> yet we considered him stricken by God,
>   smitten by him, and afflicted.
> But he was pierced for our transgressions,
>   he was crushed for our iniquities;
> the punishment that brought us peace was upon him,
>   and by his wounds we are healed.
> We all, like sheep, have gone astray,
>   each of us has turned to his own way;
> *and the* LORD *has laid on him*
>   *the iniquity of us all.*
>
> verses 4–6, emphasis added

This identification means that He, who knew no sin, *became* sin. What Jesus did was to come down to your level and take hold of your hand while you were drowning in your sin. Then He raised you up with Him to stand in His righteousness.

So when you pray for people who you know are still entangled in sin, you should not pray with an attitude that keeps you distant from their problems: "I'm the righteous one here, they are the sinners." But this prayer of identification in the Spirit reaches out to people right where they are, and by your prayers you lift them up to where they should be.

Jesus was tempted in every way, so He knows how we feel when we are tempted. In this same way, we need to allow our emotions to be touched by the pain of others so that we can identify with their needs more easily. The Bible tells us to "Rejoice with those who rejoice, and weep with those who weep" (Romans 12:15, NKJV).

Occasionally I have seen people touched by the Holy Spirit in a prayer meeting so that they will begin to weep for a person, a situation or even a nation. Afterward they have commented on how suddenly they felt this strong emotion and that it took them by surprise. In these situations, I believe that God allows us to feel either what He is feeling or what the people themselves are feeling so that we are able to identify with their pain. Either way, the weeping is more than just emotional tears; it is a powerful prayer to God.

Moses was an incredible intercessor who continually identified himself with the sins of Israel. I wonder how many pastors would like to pastor this church—the church of one million moaners! For forty years he was stuck with them in the wilderness with nowhere else to go. They wanted to stone Moses and kill him; they continually accused him; they even said they would prefer to go back and live under slavery than have his leadership. At what must have become one of the lowest points of his ministry, Moses returned from his most personal and intimate encounter with God ever, where the Lord spoke with him face-to-face, and discovered that the people had fallen into pure pagan idolatry. The people broke every rule in the house! Events reached a critical point when God could no longer tolerate their rebelliousness. You would think, after all he had endured, that Moses would be cheering God on at this point, saying, "At last, God! Go ahead and let them have it!" But no, Moses says, "No, God! Don't do it!"

> Then Moses returned to the LORD and said, "Oh, these people
> have committed a great sin, and have made for themselves a
> god of gold! Yet now, if You will forgive their sin—but if not, I
> pray, blot me out of Your book which You have written."
>
> Exodus 32:31–32, NKJV

Isn't that incredible? Moses so identified with the plight of Israel
that he said to God, "If You are going to blot these people out,
You're going to have to blot me out, too, because I'm going
with them!" Could we say that about the people who live in
our community, our city and our nation? "God, if You are
going to do something to my neighborhood, then You'll have
to do it to me as well, because I am with these people!" What a
challenge!

Identification is more than sympathy—it is a spiritual
connection. God usually touches two specific areas of our lives
as He teaches us to become people who identify with others:

▶ *Self-centeredness*

When we identify with the needs of others in prayer, our prayer
life is stretched beyond our world and our needs. God desires
that we have a Kingdom mentality—that we are more
concerned with His agenda than our own. Identification will
broaden your prayer mission and vision beyond the "me,
myself and I" barriers.

▶ *Spiritual jealousy*

When the principles of identification really grip your life, all
jealousy and spiritual competitiveness are finished. It was when
I was working with Reinhard Bonnke that I began to understand
this key of identification. Night after night I heard Reinhard
preach with passion to the huge crowds as I stood behind the
stage upholding him in prayer. More and more I began to

identify with him as he preached, almost imagining I was standing next to him, as I continued to pray. While Reinhard preached I felt that I was guarding his back; I was praying that his words would have maximum impact upon the people listening. There was no sense in which I wanted to grab the microphone and say, "I think it's my turn to give it a try now!" There was no competitiveness, just a desire to see God move.

As I identified with Reinhard through prayer, I felt a total part of what he was doing. I did not feel like a spectator; I was a participant. When, at the end of his preaching, thousands would come forward in response to the Gospel, I would feel this sense of satisfaction, *Yes! We have done it!* although I had not preached a single word! It was not about whose profile was the most prominent; it was about "us" working together for the Kingdom.

We need to grasp this sense of identification in the Church. When our pastor stands on the platform on a Sunday morning, we should not be critiquing his performance. It is not about how well he presented the Word of God, but about how we, the church, partnered with him as he preached. As a group of believers we need to learn how to stand together and work together. It is not about you or me looking good—it is about us working together to make Jesus look good!

5. Discernment

Once we have a heart that is rooted in the knowledge of the love that God has for us, motivated by compassion, crying out to God for mercy not judgment, standing alongside people— then I believe God will really trust us to see deep into the hearts of people. He will trust us with the innermost secrets of others; He will show us strongholds that need dealing with, because He knows He can trust us to handle the person correctly and kindly.

Spending time in prayer and intercession develops our spiritual "seeing" gifts. Often God will give you specific revelation about people so that you can minister to their needs more accurately. But if we share this revelation information with others inappropriately, it can really damage people. This may be done innocently, but often it becomes more like gossip than spiritual revelation. Unfortunately, many people in the Church have been damaged by intercessors whose discernment may have been accur ate, but whose hearts were not mature enough to carry the weight of their revelation. It is a tragedy when spiritual insight ends up wounding people rather than releasing them.

So here are two important lessons that every prayer warrior needs to learn:

► *Learn to keep a confidence*
As you grow in the gift of spiritual discernment, your integrity will be increasingly tested. The area of your character that will be tested most as your discernment increases is your appetite for power. Knowledge is power! So when God reveals something to you, keep it confidential. Do not use the information you possess to gain favor, power or recognition. It is not even good to say, "The Holy Spirit has shown me what that person's problem is, but I can't tell you!" That is just another way of saying, "Hey, that guy has a problem and I know what it is, but I won't tell you!" That is merely wielding your power. So, avoid spiritual power play at all costs.

► *Keep to your place of authority*
Most of the mistakes that I have made over the years have been in this area of learning to handle discernment. We need to be really careful *what we do* with the things God shows us. Once God spoke to me about a couple whose marriage was struggling and showed me exactly what the problem was. I

immediately assumed that I should approach the couple and share this information with them, so I did. My discernment was 100 percent accurate, even down to describing an incident that had happened in their home that very morning. I had all the details absolutely correct, but my timing in talking to them was completely wrong. I thought my relationship with this couple was fairly secure, but this incident nearly blew it apart. Each of them was convinced the other had phoned me and told me all about the incident that morning and so they felt betrayed by each other. The whole thing went totally wrong!

I went home and complained to the Lord, "Thanks a lot, God! I shared the word You gave me and now I'm in big trouble!" And God said to me, "I didn't tell you to go and speak to them. I didn't give you that information so you could go and counsel them. I gave you that revelation because you are My friend and I trusted you to pray." I learned an important lesson—it is important to wait for instructions before you talk outside the prayer room about what God shows you in the place of prayer.

So, having heard God speak, we need to ask, "What next Lord?" God may give you a timeframe for releasing the word, or He may simply say, "Just pray." God is well able to speak directly to the people if He wants to, but so often He just wants us to pray, and no one ever has to know that He shared those details with you. Remember, we need to become trustworthy friends of God. He should be able to speak to us as friends, knowing that we will not abuse the information He shares with us. We need to become the friends of God with whom He can share His heart.

Other characteristics

There are many other characteristics that God will develop in you as you continue to allow Him to develop you as a vessel of prayer. Remember, prayer will change your life! These characteristics include *perseverance, faith,* a growing *trust* in God's character, *childlikeness* and an increasing *authority.* But I have sought to expand on what I believe are the central characteristics of an effective prayer warrior: *love, compassion, mercy, identification* and *discernment.* In the next chapter, I want to look at one very specific style and application of prayer: prayer walking.

Prayer Walking: A Practical Guide

In this chapter I want to discuss the joy of taking prayer out onto the streets of your community. Prayer walking is a useful tool that is being used increasingly by prayer teams as they pray for their communities and reclaim their geography for the Kingdom of God. There are two questions that people often ask whenever this topic is discussed: "What is prayer walking?" and "Does praying outside have more effectiveness than praying at home?" So, let us look at these issues and ask God to stretch our prayer concepts once again!

What is prayer walking?

Prayer walking is when you allow the external environment around you to provoke you to prayer. It can be a time of very simple and spontaneous prayer that begins to flow while you are walking your dog down the streets of your city. It could be a more consistent prayer of blessing that you pray each day as you pass your neighbors' homes on the way to work. Or it can be a more organized event, when a group of people comes together and systematically walks and prays through its streets about a specific community issue that is affecting the atmosphere of the homes. I know churches that have purchased detailed maps of their areas and located the key areas of crime and domestic violence and have sent prayer patrols out into these areas to pray peace for the community. In Lincolnshire, United Kingdom, the churches have partnered with the police and the traffic-safety unit, praying specifically at places where a high incidence of accidents occur, and have seen the road-fatality statistics drop dramatically over the last three years.

Prayer walking does not only have to happen outside. You can pray in your place of work. I have a friend who worked in the financial world and once a week she arrived at her office an hour earlier than all her staff to walk through her department, praying for her colleagues' salvation and the atmosphere of the office. You could also do this, and make your walk down the corridor to the coffee machine a prayer journey for your work colleagues! When I worked at St. Bartholomew's Hospital, I would always pray for a spirit of healing to be poured out upon the patients as I walked from place to place to collect blood samples or deliver reports. I would use this walking time to pray for blessing upon the staff and for healing for the patients.

What is the purpose of praying outside?

Is praying outside more effective than praying at home? After all, the Spirit of God is not affected by distance, so what is the purpose of praying outside? When you pray outside, you find that you engage your whole being in the process of prayer. There is a greater focus of both the spiritual and physical dimensions coming together. There is a total commitment to this process of prayer and you know that your body, soul, mind and spirit all have one target of faith. I know that when I go prayer walking my whole being is engaged, my faith is stirred and I am not easily distracted. We read in the Lord's Prayer the statement that says, "Let it be on earth as it is in heaven," and as we prayer walk I have this sense that our prayers are creating an alignment between the purposes of God in heaven and this piece of earth. I imagine that my feet are the pens that begin to write the purposes of God on this piece of land and His Kingdom will come to *this* place. My feet are touching earth, but my spirit is connected to heaven, and so I become a lightning conductor that connects the will and purposes of God in heaven to this geography.

> "I will give you every place *where you set* your foot, as I promised Moses."
>
> Joshua 1:3, emphasis added

There is something awesome about putting our feet, filled with faith, on the land and releasing the presence of God. It is not just the fact that you are walking that makes the difference, but rather the faith-filled placing of your feet with Kingdom purpose that has effect. We need *to set* our feet upon the land, not just tip-toe through the tulips—we are the feet of the warrior bride!

Prayer walking also allows information and revelation to come together in a very practical way. So often we have a series of statistics available and feel that we know our locality, but when you actually visit the areas you see a different picture. You are able to see how both the natural and the spiritual atmospheres are working together. If you prayer walk the same street, both in the day and at night, you will usually get two very different perspectives. At night *all the darkness* comes out! Prayer walking stimulates the information and understanding you have and helps you pray more specifically for the needs than if you are just "thinking" about your community and praying from your church.

As you walk through the streets of a city, you can often sense the atmospheres in an area. Just one turn left can change the atmosphere from a safe, happy feeling to a violent, intimidating place. It is only as you walk the streets of the city that you are able to sense these atmospheres and pray more effectively for these areas.

Is prayer walking in the Bible?

Yes! We have the illustrations of prayer walks of intimacy with God. Both Adam and Enoch walked with God and talked. Adam and God walked together through the garden in the cool of the evening, talking with one another. There was also Enoch who walked with God and "was no more" because God took him, so maybe you should tell someone about your prayer walks with God in case you never come back!

But in Nehemiah 2 we read the story of prayer walking for a city:

> I went to Jerusalem, and after staying there three days I set out during the night with a few men. I had not told anyone what my God had put in my heart to do for Jerusalem. . . . By night I went out through the Valley Gate . . . examining the walls of Jerusalem, which had been broken down, and its gates, which had been destroyed by fire. . . . The officials did not know where I had gone or what I was doing, because as yet I had said nothing to the Jews or the priests or nobles or officials or any others who would be doing the work.
>
> Then I said to them, "You see the trouble we are in: Jerusalem lies in ruins, and its gates have been burned with fire. Come, let us rebuild the wall of Jerusalem, and we will no longer be in disgrace." I also told them about the gracious hand of my God upon me and what the king had said to me.
>
> They replied, "Let us start rebuilding." So they began this good work.
>
> Nehemiah 2:11–13, 16–18

Here we read that Nehemiah has information about the city of Jerusalem, but he takes a group of trusted friends at night and looks at the city again. He walks the boundaries of his city and discovers the extent of the broken walls and lives that live in his city.

My journey with prayer walking started in London. I had been praying for London and asking God to give me wisdom and a strategy to pray for this huge city when one morning I woke up singing this song—"Let me take you by the hand and walk you through the streets of London"! At first I did not realize it, but this was my call to prayer walking. Having just returned from Africa, I was still very intimidated by the busy streets of London, but I found a young student who lived in London and had a passion for prayer and he took me out walking. As he walked me through the streets, I found myself weeping—I looked into the eyes of the many people pushing their way along the pavements and I felt overwhelmed by their pain. The atmosphere in several areas was so dark and intimidating—but I walked in Mayfair; I walked in Hackney; I walked the streets in the day and I walked at night. In fact, I walked the streets of London regularly for a period of three months. London got into my heart and still today I cannot help but cry out to God for my capital city.

Many accounts have been written about the power of prayer walking. In Cindy Jacobs' book, *Possessing the Gates of the Enemy,*[1] she recounts the story of a church in California that used to go out on the streets with its worship band to praise. The worship began to have an effect on the surrounding area so that peace prevailed. It was so noticeable that the local police began phoning the church to ask if its members would come and worship in other areas that were known trouble spots! This is what I long to see happening in our neighborhoods. I believe that we have been given the keys of the Kingdom; we need to use these keys to unlock peace in our communities and cities. As we prayer walk we can release His power and His presence into the community.

Practical planning for your prayer walk

There are three practical steps of planning that will help you engage in the process of prayer walking. Basically they are: what you need to prepare before you go out, what you should do when you are walking and what you need to do once you return.

1. Preparation before you go out prayer walking

▶ *Decide the purpose and location*
Before deciding to go and prayer walk, ask God to show you the purpose of your prayer walking. I know God called me to go and walk the streets of London so that I would become familiar with the city and its various needs. Once you know why you are prayer walking, ask God to show you the dimensions of the geographical assignment He has given you. Maybe you already have a regular route that you walk to work that He wants you to claim as prayer walking time, or perhaps you need to get a map out and ask God to show you what are the areas of your geography that He has assigned to you to watch over. In Isaiah 62:6 it states that, "I [God] have posted watchmen on your walls" to watch over the city. I do believe that God has given us specific duties on behalf of our communities. So let God "post" you as a watchman for your geography. Listen to Him and then let Him send you out on spiritual patrol duty!

▶ *Decide on the strategy and method*
Before you leave to prayer walk, it is good to ask God to give you a strategy while you pray. Take time to look at specific

prophecies and promises given for the area. Read your Bible and ask God to give you particular verses that declare the heart of God for your area and speak them out as you walk. For example, if you know God has asked you to go and pray specifically about the violence in your neighborhood, you could prepare Scriptures to take with you. Remember, the words that you speak are like light in a dark place. So when you are looking for the verses to take with you, identify the spiritual atmosphere and then find the promises of God that demonstrate the opposite atmosphere/spirit and speak out these words over the people. If you are praying for salvation to come to your area, then you could prepare some Scriptures concerning salvation and pray them over houses as you walk by. So, you can use Scriptures both to bless and as a spiritual weapon. Psalm 149:6–9 states:

> May the praise of God be in their mouths
>   and a double-edged sword in their hands,
> to inflict vengeance on the nations
>   and punishment on the peoples,
> to bind their kings with fetters,
>   their nobles with shackles of iron,
> to carry out the sentence written against them.
> This is the glory of all his saints.

God's Word is a double-edged sword that can do serious damage to the enemy's territory. As a result of declaring it over the land, we are affecting the spiritual atmosphere of the community around us.

Hebrews 4:12–13 also speaks of the dynamic, living power of the Word:

> For the word of God is living and active. Sharper than any
> double-edged sword, it penetrates even to dividing soul and

spirit, joints and marrow; it judges the thoughts and attitudes of the heart. Nothing in all creation is hidden from God's sight. Everything is uncovered and laid bare before the eyes of him to whom we must give account.

The word *active* means that it is operative, powerful and effective. As we speak out the Word of God over the community, it hits with Holy Spirit power and does not return void, but returns to God having accomplished everything that He intended it to accomplish. When we pray with Scripture we can pray with authority because we know we are praying according to the will of God—so we hit the target every time!

► *Prepare items you need to take with you*

As you prepare your heart you may find that God gives you practical actions that He wants you to perform as you walk through the community. Be open to hear and then prepare the necessary items. You may want to break bread and share Communion within your group on one of the high places near your town and so will need to take the bread and wine. You may want to mark maps with observations as you walk. You may feel that you want to put stakes into the ground that carry the promises of God. All these items will need to be prepared and taken with you on your walk. So be prepared!

► *Prepare information and pray for discernment*

As we prepare to walk into the community, we need to be aware that we must train both our spiritual and natural eyes and ears to "hear" what both God and the land are saying. Prepare some information before your walk so that you have a general grasp of the geography, statistics of the areas and outline history. Take time to research the meaning of significant place names in the area and discover if the city has a motto or special dates or customs. Then with this knowledge ask God to increase your sensitivity to discern the spiritual atmospheres. Expect God to show you "hidden" information about your area. Keep your eyes and ears open to find this information. Take time to listen to God in the private place so that in the public place you will hear His voice more easily. Remember, the Holy Spirit can be like a metal detector; when you get near a problem an alarm sets off in your spirit, and you need to learn to listen to this warning sound and know what it means!

2. Actions and attitudes while prayer walking

Now that you are out on the streets prayer walking, what should you do and how should you behave?

▶ **Walk out knowing God is with you**

Remember you are on Kingdom business, responding to heaven's call and so you walk out as His ambassador with diplomatic status in your community. So walk, confident that God is with you, and that He has given you authority over the land where you place your feet. Joshua 1:9 says,

> "Have I not commanded you? Be strong and courageous. Do not be terrified; do not be discouraged, for the LORD your God will be with you wherever you go."

As you walk in faith, remember that God will protect and help you. So do not let fear or intimidation confuse your mind, but walk knowing God is with you and will anoint you to pray effectively.

▶ **Declare the "God" purpose over the area**

As you walk in your area, be aware of the research that you have done and declare the heavenly purpose connected to the name or mottos you have found. For many years I lived near Hemel Hempstead, in Hertfordshire. I discovered that this name was derived from the German meaning "heavenly homesteads." The statistics show that Hemel Hempstead has anything but heavenly homes, so when we prayer walked this area we declared the redemptive purpose of God on this community and prayed that the homes would reflect heaven! Ask the Holy Spirit to reveal the redemptive purpose of your area to you—in other words, declare over the land what it should be like if fully yielded to God's agenda.

Often you can use the Scriptures or promises you know God has given you in your times of preparation and speak these out. I know I often use this Scripture in Britain as I feel this is a promise for our nation:

> "Arise, shine, for your light has come,
>   and the glory of the LORD rises upon you."
>
> Isaiah 60:1

I speak it over the community, praying that it will arise to its Christian heritage once again!

▶ *Keep connected to Jesus*

As you are prayer walking, remember to stay connected to Jesus and surround yourself with an attitude of worship and praise. Do not be afraid to sing to yourself and declare His praises in the streets—you do not have to sing at the top of your voice! This proclamation of praise is like a sharp sword that helps pierce through the spiritual darkness. Pray and declare the Scriptures you have prepared beforehand. It is good to have written them down so they are accessible, unless you have memorized them.

▶ *Speak blessing on the community*

Keep a happy face as you walk, smile and be ready to talk to people if they stop you. Do not look intense and religious! As people pass you, pray a prayer of blessing for them. Try to pray more than "God bless them"—pray for peace, for joy, and so on. As you watch them approach you, ask God to show you about their needs. Bless the people of your community with the love of Jesus as you pass them in the street. I would recommend that it is best if you do this silently!

▶ *Ask for angelic protection for your community*

In Hebrews we read this verse:

> Are not all angels ministering spirits sent to serve those who will inherit salvation?
>
> Hebrews 1:14

I believe that as people who have been saved, we can ask God to send angels to assist us in our community work! I believe that the natural and the spiritual realms need to work in alignment and that God loves deploying angels to help us do our Kingdom work. We need the angelic security guard on duty on our streets!

▶ *Pray for the economic climate of your area*

As you walk and pray, notice the significant business institutions and industry in your area. Make a note of these on your map. Remember, if large factories close or shopping areas fail economically, people lose their work and the whole area suffers. So we need the blessing of God upon the finance and industry in the area. Some friends of mine in Utica, New York, have really prayed for their area after three major companies closed. They began to speak jobs and success to the area, and now some new major clients are moving their businesses into the area, providing the jobs that were lost. The city is coming out of poverty!

▶ *Take time to stop and ask for revelation*
As you walk the streets, take time to pause and just watch! Remember, every face holds a life, and every door tells a story. Ask the Holy Spirit to give you words of knowledge that will help you pray intelligently for the area in the future.

▶ *Bless the churches*
As you walk your area bless the churches as you see them. Read their notice boards and discover a little of their interests. Find the minister's name and pray for him, and remember to thank God for the diversity of the Christian expression you have in your area. Ask God to show you how to pray for each church and pray that they will grow. Also take a note of the other religious institutions in your area.

▶ *Be ready for divine appointments*
One day I went prayer walking through Watford town center. I had my plans but as I neared the top of High Street I met a work colleague from five years ago. Immediately she touched my arm and said, "Rachel, I cannot believe this! I was just thinking about you!" She then shared that her mom was ill and she was on her way to the hospital, but she was so frightened her mom would die. God gave me the opportunity to pray with her, reconnect my friendship for a season and then help her through her time of loss. So be ready for those unusual meetings and be prepared to change all your well-intentioned plans!

3. You have returned—so what next?

► *Pause for a moment and give thanks*
Take a moment just to reflect on the goodness of God. So often you feel so full of inspiration and information after a time of prayer walking that you just need to pause! Then go over the walk in your mind and just thank God for all the little details that He showed you. Even if you cannot see any immediate tangible effects from your walk, trust and know that your prayers will have a harvest.

► *Protect the seed you have sown*
Every prayer that you have prayed is like a seed of promise lying on the ground of your community. Pray that God would protect these "seeds" of prayer that you have sown. Often we do not see the answers immediately, but watch the local newspapers and wait to see what will happen. You may see the headlines of a major drug haul on an estate and realize that this was where you had just been praying and declaring, "Let light come into the darkness"! This is what happened to some of my friends after they had been prayer walking in Liverpool, United Kingdom. Also remember that sometimes you need to pray and take your responsibility now, so that you release a blessing for the future. Even if you do not see all the results you hoped for, remember, *now* is not a good time to give up!

► *Write a report for your journal*
Remember to write down your impressions, your thoughts as you prayed, and keep a note of any information that you collected. Also, as you were prayer walking you may have noted areas that you wanted to research further—put these comments in your action box! Remember to update your map with information that you collected. You may find that you need to

prayer walk an area more than once! If you are prayer walking as part of a group, compare your notes with others on a regular basis. If you discover themes and similarities, then take note that clearly God is highlighting these issues as being important.

▶ *Enjoy the glow of satisfaction*
Sit and just enjoy the presence of God, put your feet up, enjoy some worship music with a big cup of good coffee and let God bless you. Don't just rush into your next list of tasks but take a few minutes to absorb the thankfulness of God as He blesses you for your obedience. Well done—you have done a good job!

Testimonies from prayer walking

There is nothing like some good stories to inspire you, so enjoy these testimonies. I am grateful to Caroline Anderson, a friend of mine who inspired me afresh on this subject a few years ago and has inspired some of the content of this chapter.

Several years ago Caroline Anderson felt challenged to start prayer walking her street for a period of forty days. She lived on a large cul-de-sac, which would take perhaps ten minutes to walk around, and God asked her to walk and pray this road every day for forty consecutive days. Ten minutes a day, right on your doorstep sounds easy in theory, but she found it more challenging than she anticipated.

There were two main Scriptures that Caroline felt the Holy Spirit prompted her to use: Malachi 4:5–6, which speaks about restoring relationships—turning the hearts of fathers to their children, and the hearts of children to their fathers—and Philippians 2:10, which speaks of every knee bowing at the name of Jesus. As she and her husband walked the street together, they worshiped and prayed specifically for their neighbors' marriages.

About twenty days into this prayer-walking season, Caroline visited a neighbor who was separated from her husband and lived alone, but when Caroline knocked at her door, her husband answered. Surprised, Caroline went in and had coffee with the lady and during the course of the conversation she told Caroline, "Do you know, I really believe in marriage and family now. My husband and I are getting back together again." Some people might call this a coincidence, but I believe this restored relationship was a direct result of Caroline's prayer walking. For twenty days she had passed that lady's door, praying out these Scriptures about restoring relationships, and now a change was taking place in this home.

Farther down the road there was a young boy who lived in a Christian home, but he was pretty rebellious. During this forty-day season his behavior changed markedly, even his face and his whole countenance changed and finally he decided to recommit his life to Jesus.

Six months later another man told Caroline that during the time when she had been prayer walking the street, his relationship with his son suddenly, for no apparent reason, dramatically improved after being strained for a long time. This is real prayer in action! People can be radically changed and decide to choose God without us even talking to them!

Further hints and practical helps

Some more quick points for thought:

- There is power in unity, especially when people from different churches partner together to pray for the area. Are there Christians in your neighborhood from other churches who would join you in prayer walking?

- Pray for people by name. Try to find out the names of your neighbors (you can usually get this information from your library where you can get access to the electoral roll) so that you can pray for them by name.

- Take a map and track where you pray so that you know when you have covered every street. You can ask different groups to take responsibility for different areas.

- Climb up a hill or go to a high point (top of a building) that overlooks the town, and write a declaration and pray it over the area. You can write your own personal declaration for your situation or adapt the following prayer, written by Caroline Anderson, for your town.

> Father, we thank You for every man, woman, teenager and child in _____ , and we ask You that they will find a relationship with You, Jesus. We ask that You would destroy all unbelief that works in their lives so that they will be free to believe. We bind every work of the evil one that would stop the advancement of the Kingdom of God today. We declare that Jesus is the Lord of _____ and that at the name of Jesus, every knee must bow in _____ . We ask for Your Kingdom to be extended today, for the town to be known for its righteousness and justice, for its compassion, unconditional love, integrity and honesty, for these are the values of Your Kingdom, and we ask for Your Kingdom to come in _____ today as it is in heaven. We speak these values into the local government, the hospital, the schools and every shop, office and home; every factory, business and church. We declare it to be a heavenly place in Jesus' name. Amen.

- Pray Kingdom values into your community. If Jesus was the chairman of your local government, what sort of place would He make your town? What sort of community would He want to develop? What things would He allow in and what things would He keep out of your town? Start to pray for those things and find relevant Scriptures to underpin your prayers.

- After soaking your community in prayer, begin to seek God for one specific area where there needs to be a breakthrough. It could be a failing school or poor community care that you are concerned about. Ask the Holy Spirit to reveal God's strategy for that situation and begin to persistently pray into it.

Prophetic acts and prayer walking

Sometimes God asks us to accompany our prayers with specific actions. These are often called *prophetic acts*. We see an example in 2 Kings 2:19–22, where Elisha took salt to "heal" a polluted water supply.

> The men of the city said to Elisha, "Look, our lord, this town is well situated, as you can see, but the water is bad and the land is unproductive."
>
> "Bring me a new bowl," he said, "and put salt in it." So they brought it to him.
>
> Then he went out to the spring and threw the salt into it, saying, "This is what the LORD says: 'I have healed this water. Never again will it cause death or make the land unproductive.'" And the water has remained wholesome to this day, according to the word Elisha had spoken.

Elisha threw salt into the bad water as a prophetic act, physically demonstrating that God was speaking and would cleanse the water supply. In the same way, there are times when we may use prophetic acts to signify or underline something God has revealed to us in prayer. Sometimes people will anoint the lintels of their house with oil, representing the Holy Spirit. Others may pour out red wine or red grape juice onto the land to signify the cleansing and protecting power of the blood of Jesus. People may still throw salt into rivers to cleanse the spiritual atmosphere, but remember none of these actions will have any power if they are not accompanied with faith and prayer.

So remember, if you do feel God prompting you to demonstrate a prophetic act while prayer walking, make sure that anyone who is with you understands what you are doing and why you are doing it, so that you can come into a place of agreement, faith and unity. If the act is just a ritual, it will have no effect or power, but if used correctly prophetic acts can be incredible spiritual tools in prayer.

Taking responsibility for the land

There is a sobering verse in Jeremiah 12:11 that says,

> "The whole land will be laid waste
> because there is no one who cares."

Or another translation says, "... no one who takes it to heart." We need to let this Scripture touch our hearts. We need to know that we have a real responsibility to care for the welfare of our land. In Deuteronomy 11:12 we see a similar theme:

> It is a land the LORD your God cares for; the eyes of the LORD your God are continually on it from the beginning of the year to its end.

This verse, of course, refers to Israel entering the Promised Land, but I believe it is also true for my community, your community. God's eyes are still upon all He has created and He cares deeply about it. God created this geography and He wants us, His children, to take responsibility to pray for the land, to walk on it and proclaim God's Kingdom on earth.

In Acts 17:26 we read that our geographical location is destined by God:

> "From one man he made every nation of men, that they should inhabit the whole earth; and he determined the times set for them and the exact places where they should live."

So God has placed you in your community for a purpose: to reach out to others and bring the blessing of God upon them. So now you need to put on your diplomatic uniform and get out onto the streets and begin walking and praying! Then you will begin to see God move in your community, the atmosphere will change and the land will be reclaimed for the glory of God.

Note
1. Cindy Jacobs, *Possessing the Gates of the Enemy* (Grand Rapids: Chosen Books, 1994).

Persistent Prayer: *Now* Is *Not* a Good Time to Give Up!

However much we hate conflict, most of us have to admit we do have a stubborn streak when it comes to certain things we feel strongly about. Unfortunately, we tend to be stubborn about the wrong things rather than the right things! All of us have the ability to dig our heels in and say, "No, I don't want to." If only we would apply the same kind of stubbornness to our prayer lives, so that once we began praying for something we didn't easily give up. God wants us to have that kind of tenacity, a godly stubbornness when we pray. It is what the Bible calls *persistent prayer*. Many times in our prayer lives we struggle with being persistent, yet endurance is an essential prayer quality. So in this chapter let God awaken your stubbornness for breakthrough. Remember, now is not a good time to give up!

Once when I was speaking at a conference in Seattle, a lady came and spoke to me. She told me that she had been walking through a shopping mall when she spotted a jacket and felt that God wanted her to buy it for someone as a special gift. When she arrived at the meeting and heard me speak, she immediately knew, *That jacket is for Rachel.* So she asked me, "Can I give you the money to go and buy this jacket?" So I went and bought it, and I call it my "harvest" jacket because of the pattern of ears of wheat in its design. As soon as I laid eyes on it, God spoke to me and said, "It is going to be like a prophetic coat to you. You are going to wear the jacket as a declaration that it is harvest time."

We all want to reap the harvest of our prayers, don't we? We patiently sow seeds of prayer and expect that in due course, they will bear fruit and we will reap a harvest. I believe God is saying prophetically that the harvest time is coming for *stubborn* prayers—those long-term prayers that you have prayed and prayed and nothing has seemed to happen. I am sure you have these sorts of prayers in your life. Have you ever prayed for something over and over and instead of things getting better they seemed to get worse? Instead of receiving the break-through, your situation became more impossible until you thought, *God, what are You doing here?* If that is true for you, then God wants to make a declaration to you now: Praying time is never wasted time. There is going to be a harvest from your prayers. Every place where you have sown your prayers, especially with tears, the harvest is going to come.

Maturing in our prayer lives

I believe in these days God is calling the Church to a new place of responsibility and maturity in prayer. We have heard the cry of the Holy Spirit saying, "Come on, Church, it's time to grow up; time to take responsibility; time to take hold of your promises." We have wanted to stay and enjoy being little children of God, and that's right—we are always children of God—but we should not remain spiritual toddlers, never accepting our responsibility and the destiny call upon our lives.

But now it is time to grow up and take responsibility. We cannot stay on milk any longer and have Daddy doing every-thing for us! Just because we grow up and take responsibility does not mean we have to lose the intimacy of our Father. My daughter, Nicola, married eighteen months ago, but she is still her daddy's little girl, and Gordon and Nicola have a wonderful relationship. She has left home and now carries new responsibilities in her life; she has grown up but she is still our child! In the same way, we are children of the Kingdom but we have got to get busy about our Father's business. Our Father has given us a mandate and a commission and *now* is the time to carry the Good News of the Kingdom to our communities.

Jesus came and *worked* while He was on the earth. He completed His mission and declared, "It is finished." He has risen to the right hand of the Father, and handed the baton to us, so whose job is it to declare the Good News on the earth now? Yours and mine! Jesus made the way for us and set an example for us to follow. He has now given this mandate to us.

God spoke to me recently about this area: He said that He wants His Church to come to a place of responsibility with *consistency*. In other words, God wants us to stick in there with our prayers. Sometimes we have seasons in prayer when we are focused and determined, and we push through, but often we simply give up and check out, even when we have not finished our task. In the past I have led prayer teams and after a few months suddenly noticed several people have disappeared. I would occasionally ask people why they stopped attending and they would often respond, "Oh, well, I wasn't sure I wanted to do that anymore. I thought I would try something else." Instead of being led by our emotions or the next "good idea," we need to learn to be persistent and consistent. We are good starters but we must learn to be good finishers as well. Jesus is the Alpha and the Omega, the beginning and *the end*!

Everyone knows that commitment and responsibility work together. Take marriage, for instance. You cannot commit yourself to the covenant of marriage and still expect to have no

responsibilities! With the commitment comes a level of responsibility. I might wake up one morning and think, *I don't feel like
being a wife today.* As a matter of fact, that often happens when I
look at the ironing pile! *Why can't I be single again, then I won't
have to iron all these shirts!* Well, whether I feel like it or not,
I have a responsibility because I made a commitment! How
many parents wake up on a Saturday morning and think, *Today
I would love to sleep late and be childless again. I don't want to have
to get up and fix breakfast for the kids?* But whether you want to or
not—you have responsibilities.

Similarly, many people do not really enjoy their work, but
they have bills to pay and so off to work they go. In fact, most of
us do something we do not like every day of our lives. So why
do we do it then? Because we have understood that our
responsibility goes *beyond our personal preference and desires.*
We need to see this in the Church; we need to realize that we
have spiritual responsibilities, mandates from God that we need
to fulfill whether we feel like it or not.

Consistent prayer mixed with faith

So in these days God is calling us to be an army of mature
pray-ers who are consistent and persistent. Sometimes prayer
does feel like hard work—it is just a committed routine of
diligent, hard work for the Kingdom. We do not only pray when
we feel goose bumps; we do not pray because we feel anointed;
we pray because we have been commanded to pray. We just do
it! God is looking for that resolute consistency in His army—that
we pray without ceasing; we hold fast and we don't give up.

We need to be continually seeking our Father's face, saying,
"God, we've got nowhere else to go! We are committed to
staying with You!" My friend John Pressdee speaks about being
obedient to God in prayer. All of us can remember a time in our

life when we obeyed our parents' wishes, even though we wanted to do something totally different. We did not obey our parents because *we felt like it*, we just obeyed because of *our respect for their authority*. There are times when it is the same in the Kingdom of God—you just need to obey. Obedience has power. If God has asked you to do certain things for Him, then do not wait until you feel emotionally moved—just make a decision. Do it because God has told you to.

Hebrews 6:10 promises us,

> God is not unjust; he will not forget your work and the love you have shown him as you have helped his people and continue to help them.

Here I am using this verse in a slightly different context. So I would like us to reflect on it in relation to our service of prayer. When we pray for others we are "serving" them. God is not unjust. He does not forget that service. The writer of Hebrews continues,

> We want each of you to show this same diligence to the very end, in order to make your hope sure. We do not want you to become lazy, but to imitate those who through faith and patience inherit what has been promised.
>
> Hebrews 6:11–12

When praying for something, we can often start off with a great sense of enthusiasm, but then it peters out. We need to finish with the same sense of diligence. Faith and patience win the day. It is time for that consistent prayer, mixed with faith.

God spoke this to me one morning: "Rachel, usually unanswered prayer is not a wrong prayer, just an unfinished one." Sometimes we pray into a situation and when nothing happens, we give up. We think that nothing has changed because we are not praying correctly. It is more likely that we simply have not prayed long enough, and we need to push all the way to breakthrough.

Now is *not* a good time to give up!

Galatians 6:9 says,

> Let us not become weary in doing good, for at the proper time we will reap a harvest if we do not give up.

Your prayer life is most probably a lot more effective than you realize, so never grow weary of doing good! The enemy would have you believe that the delay in the answers to your prayers is due to you being a bad person, or not knowing how to "pray right." In actual fact, your prayers are having an untold effect in heaven and on earth. You are probably praying the right prayers, but you just need to keep praying persistently until you see the answer.

One of the most common pitfalls in prayer is *weariness*. Most of us, if we look back at situations we prayed for, will see, "Yes, I got really tired in that season and gave up praying." That is why it is so important to have relationships in the place of prayer; that is why we need good prayer groups and prayer partners. We need people to cheer us on. We need people to say, "Hey! You are doing good!" If we seek to help one another in prayer, to minister encouragement, then it will be much easier to complete that course.

The miracle of prayer is that it brings about an alignment between the spiritual and the natural. Things decreed in heaven need to be "pulled" down and established on the earth through prayer. When that process is complete, the answer to our prayer arrives. It is what the apostle Paul calls "the fullness of time" or the "proper" time. It is a God-ordained *kairos* moment when heaven and earth touch and we see the breakthrough we need. As we begin to pray, we start the process of this alignment between the spiritual and the natural, so eventually at the "proper" time we will receive the harvest of our prayers.

Until we have the breakthrough, we need to "mind the gap." Anyone who has traveled on the London underground trains will have heard the voice over the loudspeaker system, constantly reminding the people, "Mind the gap, please! Mind the gap, please!" as the doors open and people get on and off. In the same way God is speaking to His intercessors and calling them to "mind the gap" because there is a gap between heaven and earth; a void between what God has declared to be and what we see in reality at this time on the earth. Look at any situation and you will see this is true; look at what's happening in your local community, for instance: There is a gap between what God wants for your community and the reality. Heaven is declaring, "Let His Kingdom come," but earth is out of alignment. Prayer, then, is like a spiritual workout. With one hand we are laying hold of heaven's desire and with the other, earth's reality, and we need to pull the two together in prayer. We pray, "Lord, let Your Kingdom come to *this* place." It can take a lot of pulling to bring about that alignment, but once you have heard your instruction from the Lord, you need to declare this over your community, saying, "Lord, this community will see Your salvation," for instance. You touch the throne of God for that area; you take God's prophetic word He has spoken over that place—heaven's proclamation. There is a gap and you have to close this gap with the arms of faith.

If you have connected with heaven in this way and you are pulling, pulling, but then you let go too soon, what happens? You miss the opportunity of the breakthrough you were looking for. But if you *persist* in prayer, then at the "proper" time you will reap the harvest. Sometimes everything seems to shout around you, "Don't bother; give up. You're a failure!" But you need to become stubborn and refuse to give up your place of prayer. Something inside of you needs to cry out, "No! I'm not going to give up!"

Following the accident I described in chapter 3, I returned home from Africa in November 1984 in a wheelchair, burning with a word that God was going to heal my legs. My faith expectation level was high because I had just been healed from multiple fat emboli, which nearly killed me. In the light of this, I did not think it would take long for God to heal my legs, but after a month, nothing had happened. In fact, things got worse. I was in constant pain and the fractured bones were not knitting together as they should. I was going back and forth to the hospital where they were constantly telling me, "Nothing is happening. Your legs are so badly crushed that there isn't enough blood supply for the bones to knit back together."

I had been in plaster for six months with no callus forming, so the doctors wanted to take me into the Royal Stanmore Orthopedic Hospital to do several bone grafts. These bone grafts would involve a nine-month process where a surgeon would remove bone from my hip and pack the bone chips into my damaged legs, and then give me time to recover before performing the same procedure on the other leg. I was not delighted at that prospect.

I thank God for church in times like this! The precious group of four churches in Hertfordshire where I lived— Hemel Community Church, Watford Community Church, Garston Community Church and St. Albans Community Church—organized a number of "Warring Praise" evenings. They would come together and repeatedly lay hands on me and pray for my legs. I longed for them to be healed instantaneously, but they were not. It felt like the bones were moving a fraction of an inch every time they were prayed for, but at least they were moving! With every concerted prayer effort came a little breakthrough.

However, my progress also seemed to falter and regress, so it was decided more concentrated prayer would be needed. It was a constant battle, but my dear friends wrestled for me in prayer. After some sixteen months I was able to actually stand on my legs. Eventually the plaster casts came off and I was able to stand with just leg supports. As soon as I was able to bear weight we returned to Zimbabwe, Africa, in January of 1986. I still was not able to walk very easily and certainly could not bear weight for any length of time; after only five minutes my muscles would be exhausted. However, I clung to my promise that God had given me after I woke up from the coma. It was based on Hebrews 12:13:

> Make a straight path for your feet. Steady those legs, for the lame will no longer be called disabled, but rather, healed.

I knew this was the Word of God to me—it was not just my little thought for the day. This was not a "good idea" but "God's idea" for my life! But after eighteen months I was frustrated, thinking, *God, we want to serve You! We want to work for You in Africa!* Surely, since God wanted us to work in Africa, He had to heal me? But still we did not have the breakthrough.

Regardless of this, we decided to return to Africa and continued working with Reinhard Bonnke. I was not able to walk easily because my right leg was significantly shorter than my left. The muscle at the back of my leg was tethered to my tendons so it meant that my right heel didn't touch the ground. It also meant I had a very twisted foot that turned inward. I could not walk downstairs easily and I found it very difficult to maintain my balance.

Here we were, working with Reinhard—one of the most incredible healing evangelists—and seeing numerous cripples healed, as well as blind eyes opened and many other miracles. After our missions I witnessed bonfires where people would burn walking sticks and crutches they no longer needed. Yet I was not healed myself. In fact, I was personally praying for people and seeing God miraculously heal them and I still was not healed!

At that time, I wanted to get pregnant and have our second child, but all the doctors advised me not to do it, concerned that my legs would not take the extra weight. But I just kept thinking, *God gave me a promise . . . the lame will no longer be called disabled.* Then I reasoned if I did get pregnant, maybe this would force the situation so God would *have* to heal me so I could carry the baby! And, indeed, a short while later I did become pregnant with our second child. But how many of us know that we cannot just manipulate God in that way? God was gracious and I got through the pregnancy okay, but still my legs were not healed.

Then almost four years after the accident, in January 1988, we were ministering in the Philippines with Reinhard Bonnke and found ourselves attending a meeting with Frances and Charles Hunter, who have a renowned healing ministry. I was not in the best spiritual frame of mind. In fact, I was exhausted and only attended the meeting very reluctantly, but Gordon had insisted we go in order to represent Reinhard who was elsewhere at the time. I said, "I don't need another meeting," but I went, leaving my heart and soul in bed at home.

While at the meeting, Charles Hunter approached me and asked very specifically if there was anything wrong with me as a result of a traffic accident. I responded, "Yes, it's my legs." At that moment my emotions were running wild. Half of me wanted to yell out, *Yes, God! At last I'm going to be healed!* But at the same time and perhaps more strongly, a wave of dread washed over me that said, *Oh no, God, please, don't play with me. I can't bear it if nothing happens! I know You gave me a word, but I can't stand the fact that it doesn't seem to be working out. I don't understand the delay; it doesn't make sense; it was so clear to me when You spoke, but what if nothing happens? I've felt this sense of hope before, but if I trust, how do I know I will not be disappointed again?*

I remember Charles put his hand on my leg and prayed for me. I desperately wanted to feel something, but I felt nothing. *Oh no, not again, please,* I cried inwardly. There were perhaps six hundred people in the room at this time and I was longing for something to happen. Then Charles said to me, "Now do something you couldn't do before I prayed." The one thing that had been impossible for me to do was to stand upright with both feet on the ground without any shoes on my feet. So very slowly and apprehensively I took my shoes off, first the left, then the right, wondering if both heels would touch the ground. I will never forget that night. As I removed my shoes, both heels *touched* the ground, and I knew the sound of my feet touching the carpet was a mighty sound of breakthrough! I stood and wept—I was completely healed!

I want to say to you that there is a mystery in prayer. There is a mystery concerning the timing of God and there is often a delay process in God's promises and their fulfillment—a mystery in understanding God's specific word to you. But do not get offended and give up. We have got to become persistent pray-ers. Just because the path to the fulfillment of the promises of God does not seem to make sense, that does not mean you are wrong. Do not grow weary of doing good. If you know you have heard from God, then hold on to it; do not change course because of the delay. Too often we allow the delay to alter the passion and focus of what we have heard and try to make the word fit our circumstances. No! Hold fast to the word. As the writer of Hebrews said, keep the same diligence to the end that you had in the beginning.

Praying in faith

When God first speaks to you about something, you tend to receive it innocently with faith, but the journey to the fulfillment of that word is the real test of your faith. The temptation is to subtly change what you heard God say when the answer does not seem to come quickly. If you have heard from God, then do not allow yourself the luxury of analyzing your word to make it more reasonable, thinking, *Maybe God actually meant this or that?* Instead, hold fast to the word to the end. Do not let the devil pickpocket your faith. Hebrews 11:6 says, "Without *faith* it is impossible to please God" (emphasis added). Think about that for a moment. If your prayer life is not connected to *active faith*, it cannot be pleasing to God. One of the things the devil loves to do is disconnect our faith from our prayer. But we have to pray with a constant atmosphere of *believing.* As the Scripture continues, "because anyone who comes to him [God] must believe that he exists and that he rewards those who earnestly seek him."

The devil would love you to pray religious prayers, where the words sound nice, but there is no real power because the faith connection has been lost. Without faith our sacrifice of prayer is not pleasing in the presence of God. So, we must believe that God hears our prayers, *and wants* to reward those who earnestly seek Him with an answer! The *earnestly* in this verse literally means He wants to reward us as we *diligently, persistently and consistently* seek His face with our prayers. If this faith connection is lost, then the result is just the sound of religious rhetoric. We have got to learn to wrestle in faith again and hold fast to the truth that God does hear our voice.

For this reason I have a bit of a love-hate relationship with prayer requests. Sometimes when people write down their prayer requests and give it to the prayer ministry or some other person, they do this because they fear that if *they* pray for it themselves, nothing will happen. They have this idea that if only they can get their prayer request under the nose of a prayer "superstar," then God will hear and answer. But remember, "without faith it is impossible to please God." You must believe that He hears you and will reward you if you continue to seek His face persistently.

You are usually the best person to pray for *your* needs. You will carry the passion and urgency for the problem; you will call upon God with all your heart, as you are involved. It is not about how good you are. You do not have to be a conference speaker or have written books! You can bring your cry to God and He will hear you. Of course, I believe that we need to come together as the family of God and pray for one another's issues, but that does not mean we abdicate our personal responsibility to seek God's face for our needs.

In James 5 it says,

> The prayer of a righteous man is powerful and effective.
> Elijah was a man just like us. *He prayed earnestly* that it would not rain, and it did not rain on the land for three and a half years.
> James 5:16–17, emphasis added

Isn't that wonderful? Your prayers are powerful and effective. I love the phrase, "Elijah was . . . *just like us*" (emphasis added). Elijah accomplished incredible things in his ministry, yet James says, "Elijah is no different from you. Don't make him a superstar. He was an ordinary person." Elijah prayed earnestly and look what happened: His prayers had an effect on the climate and, as a result, on the economy. You have no idea how powerful your prayers are!

Many prayers become unanswered prayers because they are abandoned prayers. So often in modern Church culture we abandon prayers that should be our ongoing responsibility. Sometimes we abandon them because they are not the "prayer of the month." There are always people who will call us to pray for different issues, so that we can become like spiritual butterflies—flitting from one prayer focus to the next. Prayer needs will come and go, but I believe we need to know what are the personal, long-term mandates God has given us in prayer. I believe we are called to consistently pray for our families, for instance. So, we need to check that we are continuing to pray for the right issues.

Do you have things that you have prayed over consistently in the past, but have now abandoned? Have you let go of some of your prayers? If so, I encourage you to go back to that "field" of prayer today and begin watering it again. The wonderful thing about the Holy Spirit is that His seed is incorruptible seed. Whatever you have invested in prayer so far will not be lost. You can revisit that field and say, "Lord, I'm sorry I gave up because I was weary. I'm coming back and I'm asking You to put a fresh grace on me to pray into this area again." Maybe you will pray for the salvation of a family member, or for someone who got saved and has now backslidden. But today you can have a fresh grace upon you to pray for that person or situation.

The law of sowing and reaping

For the remainder of this chapter I want to look more closely at the area of sowing and reaping in our prayer lives. There is a biblical law of sowing and reaping, and it applies to prayer as well as all aspects of our spiritual and natural lives. We see this principle summarized by Paul in Galatians 6:

> Do not be deceived: God cannot be mocked. A man reaps what he sows. The one who sows to please his sinful nature, from that nature will reap destruction; the one who sows to please the Spirit, from the Spirit will reap eternal life. Let us not become weary in doing good, for at the proper time we will reap a harvest if we do not give up.
>
> Galatians 6:7–9

The whole process of seedtime and harvest is such an illustration of prayer. Our prayers are seeds that we sow. We release them and they go into the "soil"—a dark place where they get covered up and disappear. For a long time nothing seems to be happening and perhaps we think, *God, what was that all about? I prayed my heart out and my prayers just disappeared into a dark place and nothing seems to have changed.*

But the Bible says, "Do not be deceived. . . . " Why does it say that? Because the fact is, we are very likely to be deceived! We are very likely to be taken in by the lies of the enemy, telling us our prayers did not work. But the Bible says, "Don't be conned—God is not mocked. Nobody makes a fool of God. The time you have invested in prayer will bring a harvest." This is true for all of our Christian life. God knows what we have done and He has a harvest waiting for us. Isn't that wonderful? He knows how you have sown financially and there is a harvest coming; He knows how you have served in love and there is a harvest coming . . . in every area of your life this is true—what you sow you reap.

Of course, this principle works in the negative realm as well. Verse 8 tells us that "the one who sows to please his sinful nature, from that nature will reap destruction." In other words, if you live a life of gossip, then you will reap an inheritance of gossip. But if you sow in the Spirit you are going to reap an eternal, spiritual inheritance. In short, if you plant apple seeds you will only get apples; if you plant a mango seed, then you will get mangos. The seed you plant determines the fruit you will harvest.

The fact of a law is this: It works *anywhere*. A scientific law will work in Africa just as well as it works in America. It is the same with biblical laws. If we sow then we shall surely reap. The law will work at *any time*. It does not matter if you are the newest Christian on the planet or if you have been a Christian for fifty years—it will work for you regardless. And the law will work for *anyone*. It doesn't matter who you are—a child or an adult, rich or poor; it will work for you.

We also need to recognize that laws work even if you do not believe in them or understand them! Take, for example, the law of gravity. You can stand on the top of the Empire State Building, declare your total disbelief in the law of gravity, and jump. What will happen? The law will work whether you believe it or not. I have heard a number of people say, "I don't believe in this sowing and reaping stuff," but yet it works! It does not even help if you say, "But I didn't know about the law! Nobody told me!" Even if you are completely ignorant of a law or do not understand it, it still works.

You can see the law of sowing and reaping working in society today. Society is sowing to its selfish, sinful appetites. So, what is society reaping as a result? We are reaping a harvest of increased selfishness, wickedness and sexual filth. That is why it is so critical that the Church does not grow weary of doing good and sows in the opposite spirit, so that the following generations can reap the good harvest we have sown.

Time delays

Just as in the natural, so in the spiritual there is a time delay between sowing and reaping. We do not immediately see the results of our prayers. Just as different seeds have different germination times, so in the Spirit different prayers have different harvest seasons. We all tend to behave like kids growing little beans for a science project—we put the seed in and want some results the next day! Unfortunately, most seeds take a lot longer than that to grow! We have to trust that, in the dark times of delay, our seeds of prayer are growing and God will bring the harvest at the right time.

In Luke 18 there is the wonderful parable of the widow who stood before a judge. It says specifically that,

> Jesus told his disciples a parable to show them that they should *always pray and not give up*.
>
> Luke 18:1, emphasis added

Jesus gave us this parable to underline the fact that we should not give up. The parable tells of a widow who comes before an unjust judge and keeps knocking on his door time and again saying, "Please give me what I need ... please give me what I need...." In the end, even though the judge does not want to do it, he says, "For goodness' sake, will someone sort that woman out and give her what she wants?"

That was the story that Jesus used to illustrate persistent prayer! The Bible tells us that the judge was not even a decent or an honest one—he was unjust. But we have a just, righteous, wonderful Father. Jesus says, "If this is what can happen with an unjust judge who doesn't fear God—if even his heart can be turned to give you what you want—how much more will your heavenly Father's heart be turned toward you? So come on, don't give up!"

But later, there is a very telling statement:

> "And will not God bring about justice for his chosen ones, who cry out to him day and night? *Will he keep putting them off?"*
>
> Luke 18:7, emphasis added

Have you ever thought that God "puts you off"? There are seasons when God appears to withhold Himself and almost seems to push us away. *"Will He keep putting them off?"* Why would God want to do that to us? I believe it is so we can learn to wrestle in faith. From time to time, God gives us some spiritual exercises to stretch our faith. He invites us to press in, but then holds us at arm's length and delays the answer for a little bit. It is as if God wants to test us by asking, "How much do you really want this?" He wants us to learn to battle and wrestle so that our faith will grow as a result. God does not want to keep putting you off, because His heart is to give you what you need, but He also knows that your faith needs to be stretched and grown. Time delays should help you develop your "muscles of faith" in the place of prayer. So do not let delay make you bitter, but trust!

Giving generously in prayer

Again we see the principle of sowing and reaping being discussed by Paul in 2 Corinthians 9:6–9.

> Remember this: Whoever sows sparingly will also reap sparingly, and whoever sows generously will also reap generously. Each man should give what he has decided in his heart to give, not reluctantly or under compulsion, for God loves a cheerful giver. And God is able to make all grace abound to you, so that in all things at all times, having all that you need, you will abound in every good work. As it is written:
>
> > "He has scattered abroad his gifts to the poor;
> > his righteousness endures forever."

This Scripture is often quoted in connection with our offering times, but I believe that this principle is applicable to prayer also. We should give generously in the place of prayer. Whoever sows sparingly, reaps sparingly. What sort of harvest do you want from your prayer life? Most of us want an abundant harvest; we want to pray and see lives, situations, even cities changed by God's power. Well, if a farmer wants to see a great harvest he has to plant a lot of seed, so if you want a mighty harvest from your prayer life, then you are going to have to plant a lot of seeds in prayer. You cannot expect to have mighty breakthroughs in your life if you only pray a couple of times a month. What you sow, you reap. It is a principle.

But the wonderful thing about this principle is that you always reap with *multiplication*. Your answers will always come back to you multiplied by God. So even if you are praying for a "big" situation, you don't have to pray huge prayers, you just have to consistently put your small seeds in the ground.

Verse 7 of this passage says,

> Each man should give what he has decided in his heart to give, not reluctantly.

Each of us needs to decide: What am I committed to praying for? What am I called to pray for? And then do it with joy. We must not moan and groan about it, but make a joyful sacrifice and go to the place of prayer. At times it will be hard work. There will definitely be times when you just have to decide: "I'm going to give this to the Lord. I don't really feel like it, but I have made a decision to persistently, consistently give this time of prayer to God." You might even tell God, "Lord, I don't feel like I'm doing a good job today, but I have signed up. I am going to stand in Your house of prayer at this time. Lord, I ask for Your grace to be upon me." It does not matter if your language is not perfect, your very presence in that place of prayer before God has an effect. So make a decision you are going to do it.

In Proverbs 20:4 we see this insightful verse:

> A sluggard does not plow in season;
> so at harvest time he looks but finds nothing.

Sometimes people come to me and complain, "None of my family is saved. God never does anything for me." I usually ask, "How often do you pray for them?" to which they sometimes respond, "Oh, I've given up praying for them. I used to pray but I don't bother anymore...." Well, let's take a reality check here! If you do not sow, then you will not reap. If you are expecting to see a harvest in a particular field, then you need to make sure you are sowing something so that it can grow!

Imagine how foolish it would be for a person to rant and rave to his friend about the fact that there are no plums in his garden that year, while his neighbor's garden is full of them—yet that person does not have any plum trees in his garden to begin with! You would think he was nuts! But isn't that what we do in the Church so often? We get jealous of one another—jealous of how God is blessing another person. Perhaps God is really blessing him or her financially while we are in need. At that point you need to ask yourself, *Have I been planting any trees in my garden?* This Scripture in Proverbs is saying: You can't go out at harvest time expecting to reap something if you have never planted anything! So I want to ask, what are you sowing?

Promising to pray

Lastly, I would like to consider the issue of making promises or commitments to pray. In Bible language, have you made "vows" to others and if so, are you keeping them? Ecclesiastes 5:4–5 says,

> When you make a vow to God, do not delay in fulfilling it. He has no pleasure in fools; fulfill your vow. It is better not to vow than to make a vow and not fulfill it.

We need to be diligent in keeping our commitments to pray for others and do it cheerfully. If you do not feel you can promise to pray for a person or a situation, then do not put yourself under pressure—do not promise! Often people will come up to me at the end of a conference and ask, "Please, will you pray for my daughter who is not saved?" So what I have begun to say is, "I will pray with you now, but I really can't promise to put you into my regular prayer schedule. What I will promise you is this: If God reminds me of your situation, I will pray for you." This is true of promise: It is better not to make a promise to pray than to make a promise and not keep it. We can quickly sign up for all sorts of prayer lists and later think, *Help! I actually can't do that!*

Our heart of compassion can easily outrun our actual ability to give, so be careful what you commit yourself to pray for. Maybe you even need to go back and look at some of your prayer fields and ask God, "Lord, should I still be committed to these?" Just as you might review your finances and how you give every now and again, so you need to review your "prayer giving" from time to time, asking God which fields you are still to sow into. We need God to speak to us about this because faith comes by hearing the Word of God. If we are to pray consistently into our prayer fields *with faith*, then we need to know we have the mandate of God to do it. So ask God to show you where to focus your efforts.

Finally, there are some wonderful verses in Ecclesiastes 11:4–6 that tell us not to look at the skies, or the clouds, trying to determine whether it's a good time to sow (to pray) or not, because the perfect time never comes. You should still sow, still pray.

> Whoever watches the wind will not plant;
> > whoever looks at the clouds will not reap.
> As you do not know the path of the wind,
> > or how the body is formed in a mother's womb,
> so you cannot understand the work of God,
> > the Maker of all things.
> Sow your seed in the morning,
> > and at evening let not your hands be idle,
> for you do not know which will succeed,
> > whether this or that,
> > or whether both will do equally well.

My interpretation of this is simple: Do not wait for the perfect season to pray your prayers. The perfect time for prayer never comes! Praying time is never convenient time. In our busy world we will always get interrupted or distracted. That is why we need to be determined to be persistent in the place of prayer. If your attitude is always to look for the right time for prayer, then your circumstances will always dictate how and when you are going to sow. Instead make a decision—"I'm going to pray. I'm going to be a consistent person in the place of prayer." Now is the time to pray—so remember, *pray* and do not give up, and enjoy reaping the harvest!

My Church Will Be a House of Prayer!

In the first five chapters we have focused mainly on the individual's prayer life and have seen how it can be enhanced and developed. In this chapter I want to widen the focus and look specifically at some of the skills we need to develop so that our corporate prayer meetings can be dynamic gatherings.

While it is important for each of us to develop a vital one-on-one prayer relationship with God, corporate prayer must also be a fundamental part of healthy church life. Good corporate prayer meetings will encourage you to be persistent in the place of prayer. They give you the sense that others are standing with you and want to see your breakthrough, too. Also they give you an opportunity for accountability in your spiritual prayer life, so that you can improve your discipline. If you learn to pray together with others, you will be stretched to listen to the broader sound of God's heart for His people. You can pray on your own for so long, but there is something precious about having times of prayer with others.

But so many of us know that corporate prayer meetings can either be heaven or a disaster. I grew up in a Christian home and I remember that as a child some of the worst meetings I ever had to sit through were the prayer meetings! They often have a reputation for being very long and very boring. So how do we avoid dull prayer meetings? Are there ways we can lead prayer to make sure that, as far as possible, our prayer meetings are effective and alive? Are there certain things that we need to be more real and honest about? I believe so. In this chapter I hope to help you think more practically and strategically about your prayer gatherings, but if I had to sum up my advice in one phrase it would be: *Be real and not religious!*

Prayer triplets or prayer partnerships

Let us start by looking at the skills needed to establish a successful prayer triplet. "Prayer triplets" or "prayer partnerships" have become a more usual part of church life in recent years and are a powerful way to grow spiritually and learn to pray. By prayer partnerships I mean a group of three or four people who come together and pray regularly at a defined time. Although it does not need to be the same time every week, the discipline of having a fixed time usually helps the group function regularly. Prayer triplets obviously consist of three people, but you can pray with a group of four or five people, and still retain the intimate dynamic of the small-group setting.

Many of the principles that one can learn in prayer triplets or small groups will also apply for larger groups of forty or fifty people. But larger prayer celebrations involving hundreds of people will need to have a completely different style of leadership. Most of what I will write here applies to the smaller group church prayer meetings. Here are some of the principles that I believe help your small prayer groups become effective.

1. Decide on the nature and focus of the group
You first need to define why your group is coming together to pray. Each of us has certain issues that bring us alive, because we are passionate about them. Some people have a real heart

for children's work; others for overseas missions, and so on. It is sensible for people with a similar passion and commitment to form a group to pray for this area. If you gather a group with very different styles and passions, praying together can become a frustration rather than a joy. Someone may have a burden to pray for prodigals to return "home," whereas someone else wants to pray for Siberia!

Try to connect people who have a similar passion, style of expression and calling to the place of prayer in the same group. If a person who is very quiet and likes meditative, contemplative prayer joins a group where the other members are much more gregarious and outspoken, that person can have a hard time feeling like a valuable part of the group. He or she may even go home after each meeting having to repent of their critical attitudes toward the others in the group rather than the joy of a good time of prayer! Do not put yourself in a position that is stressful unnecessarily, but be real about who you are. Define the nature of your prayer life and find like-minded people to pray with.

You should not feel guilty about praying together with people that you "click" with. You often find it is just a divine connection; you do not always know why and you cannot manufacture it, but you just have a spiritual affinity with them, often instantly. Go with that flow. I do not advise starting a prayer group to sort out poor or conflicting relationships. I have known people who have said, "I don't get on that well with so and so, so maybe if we pray together it will improve our relationship." If you want to try to mend your relationship with people, it is better to take them out for lunch and start to befriend them, but do not try to use a prayer group to reconcile your relationship crisis. Once you have sorted out your relationship, you can pray together and have a wonderful, powerful group!

If you are unsure whom to pray with, ask God for direction. Ask Him, "What should I be praying for and whom should I be praying with?" and allow Him to *form* your prayer group. Do not simply act on a "good idea," but allow God to tell you what is on His heart. You may think you need to pray for this or that issue, but those things may not be on God's agenda at this time.

Once you have formed your group, let the Holy Spirit direct your prayer meetings. As prayer leaders who want to infect and influence the Church with the sound of creative prayer, we can sometimes be too directive and put our personal prayer projects on our prayer meetings. Rather, we should ask God what issues we need to carry in our prayer groups at this time or for this season.

2. Form prayer-triplet cells and train people to pray

Having outlined that you need to form prayer groups where you connect together easily and are of a similar heart, I am now going to appear to contradict myself, but this is for the purpose of training! Often people come up to me and ask me to teach them to pray. By far the best way to teach people to pray is to invite them to watch you pray! If you want to multiply both the quality and quantity of the prayer life in your church, you must be prepared to train. So you need to form small prayer cells especially for training, led by a mature and experienced prayer leader, and integrate those with a longing to pray into these groups. An approach that is sometimes tried is just to integrate inexperienced believers into an existing mature peer group and hope they learn. This often leads to frustration all around. The experienced intercessors will feel they are having to hold back on things they would normally share, aware that a less mature Christian might struggle to handle the information; and inexperienced believers might feel intimidated by the other group members and not participate as much as they would in a "safer" environment.

If you are a mature believer, then my advice is to have a "peer group" for prayer where you can easily share your life, your heart, and be accountable; then establish an additional training group in order to bring others on in their prayer lives. You can start by taking two or three people who are younger Christians, or inexperienced pray-ers, and make sure that the group is going to relate with one another well. Remember, this group is not for you to pray from your perspective, but for you to train and lead the others and to encourage them. In this group you need to use your training and leadership gifts more than your intercession gift because you are there to train, release and equip the people with you. Encourage other mature believers to do the same and establish these groups throughout the church and enjoy the privilege of investing in the next generation. That way the depth and breadth of prayer will gradually multiply throughout the church. As leaders you should encourage everyone in the church you see with leadership potential to form these training cells.

3. Keep your prayer language simple

This is especially important when you are training younger Christians to pray. We need to keep it real and obtainable, and keep our language simple. So easily our prayer meetings become religious and people suddenly start speaking with a strange voice pitch! Others have a habit of reverting into old King James mode! "O God, we thank Thee that Thou art gracious to us," and so on. But why should people change their voice and use of English to pray? Rather, we should let our language reflect the person that we really are, and come and speak to our God with a real and vulnerable but honoring attitude. If you cultivate an atmosphere where you have to sound "special" to pray, it is incredibly intimidating and does not encourage new people to participate because they do not understand the protocol.

We need to remember one of the main purposes of prayer is to gather a harvest of souls. We want lost souls found and brought into God's Kingdom. If new people come into the church and find us using strange, archaic or inaccessible language, what will that do? It will alienate them and make them feel that they cannot join in. We must keep it accessible so that when people pray, new believers can participate and get touched with the passion to pray.

We also need to create an atmosphere where people are not afraid of making a mistake. They need to know that even if they do, they will not be publicly humiliated but lovingly understood. I remember once I was in a prayer meeting and someone prayed a beautiful prayer, really heartfelt, but during their prayer said, "Father, I thank You that in the book of Hezekiah it says..." Well, of course there isn't a book of Hezekiah in the Bible, but does it really matter? We all knew what the lady meant—she meant to talk about King Hezekiah in the book of 2 Kings. God knew what she meant, too. He wrote the Book! These are not things we should worry about too much; instead, create an atmosphere in your prayer meetings where people can pray and even make a mistake, knowing others won't judge or frown at them.

People need to feel free to learn to express themselves in these smaller groups, even prophetically, and share the heart of God and experience grace as they make mistakes. I remember a new convert prophesying for the first time in a meeting, "Just as Moses crossed the ... no, when Abraham crossed ... no, oh, well, one of them did—so I am bringing My people to a place of crossing over, a place of transfer. This is a new day and I will bring you out from a place of bondage into a new day of deliverance...." Even though the facts were not perfect, the sense of what the person was hearing from God was right; he just couldn't quite remember the story! Does it mean what he was sharing was invalid? No. He was hearing the cry of God's heart, but was still learning to find an appropriate biblical knowledge to back it up.

If we are not facilitators who allow people to make occasional mistakes, we will find that people who get it wrong once will never return to the prayer meeting again. Or if they do, they will not contribute again in a hurry. But if you are prepared to risk letting things go wrong occasionally, you'll be amazed at how often everything goes right! I like to see at least 80 percent participation in all my prayer meetings, however big or small, and I feel I am not doing a good job if I see most people just sitting down without speaking for the whole meeting. Everyone should be engaged and the only way to achieve this is to make your prayer gatherings safe places for participation.

Similarly, if you are a prayer leader, it is important to ensure that people understand what is happening in the meeting at any given time. Good practical communication is a key! It is essential, therefore, to stay sensitive to what the Holy Spirit is doing and keep your eyes open sometimes! If someone in the meeting begins to groan or cry as the Holy Spirit touches him or her, you may need to explain what is happening for the benefit of any who are frightened or perplexed by it. This way you will maintain an atmosphere of openness and inclusiveness. For instance, some people may begin to weep and sob as they connect with God's heart on an issue. At this point others may be alarmed, feeling, *Help, what's happening?* Explain it! Say, "The Holy Spirit is here. What you are hearing is the sound of the Father heart of God weeping for this situation and some people are sensing this pain and so expressing that. Don't worry about this, but just join them in prayer." If you take the time to explain, then people will not feel alienated from what is taking place. At the same time, this gives people the permission to express themselves as the Holy Spirit moves them.

4. Avoid praying for too long

This single factor has probably killed more prayer meetings and prayer groups than any other. If you are an intercessor or enjoy praying by yourself, you are probably one of the worst culprits—me included! Why? Because we are passionate about prayer and have fluency when we pray, we do not realize how long we can pray without a breath! In any prayer meeting it only takes a few people with this "gift" to dominate all the available praying time so others do not get a chance to pray out loud. Those who are guilty of this need to remember: this is a prayer meeting not their turn to preach! We must serve one another in prayer, not our own agenda. If you pray for too long, it does two things.

► *It intimidates beginners*

A younger believer may listen to your long, eloquent prayer and think, *I have only one sentence! How can I pray?* He or she needs to pray, "Lord, I thank You that You are really going to touch and bless my mother," but because it seems so insignificant compared to your prayer, he or she never prays it. As prayer leaders, it is good to encourage everyone to pray out loud—break the sound barrier! So just state, "I want us all to pray just one sentence on one topic now. Let's go around the group." We all need to break the "sound barrier" of fear, because often people are terrified of praying out loud. But a one-line prayer is manageable for everyone.

► *It does not leave any space for others*

Praying as a group is about interaction, so in order to get that dynamic you need to allow space for it. Good small-group prayer requires a different set of disciplines than praying alone. You have to leave space for others to pray. Experienced pray-ers who have prayed together for a season tend to be very good at connecting and following each other's prayers without a gap. They pick up on what is happening prophetically and go for it. But this does not give a chance for less experienced pray-ers to add their prayer. I suggest that mature prayer warriors should count to ten after the previous person's "Amen" before launching into the next prayer themselves, especially if they have already prayed in the group. This forces you to leave space for others and gives them the opportunity to join in. There is nothing more embarrassing for a person who has summoned up the courage to pray out loud, than someone more experienced cutting in at the same time and going off on a lengthy prayer! It takes some discipline for those who love to pray to leave that space, but it is a skill worth developing in order to encourage others to participate. It is all part of making prayer meetings exciting and accessible for others.

5. Give time to share revelation

Taking time to share things that God is revealing to people is an important part of corporate prayer and will need to be handled differently, depending on the size and maturity of the group. It is easier to share revelation in a prayer triplet, for instance, because of the intimacy that size of group allows. In larger settings it is more important to keep a closer eye on these contributions, as the meeting can get lost if too many people go off on tangents. We need to train people to recognize that when we come together God speaks, but not every revelation is for the public place.

It is good when there is clear revelation and direction given by the Spirit in the corporate prayer meeting. This can give the meeting a sense of faith and purpose where people know they are praying God's agenda. Otherwise, it is too easy to have prayer meetings where we each bring our own lists of favorite topics and we randomly pray about everything and anything, but it is more the noise of people talking than the faith-filled sound of radical prayer. If this is how your prayer meetings function, then you will find that it is more difficult to pray strategically and build towards something tangible. For this reason, I really believe one of the keys to effective prayer is good administration. We need to be organized.

So have a definite focus to your prayer gatherings, but then allow time for people to share prophetic revelation on the subject at hand. There are various ways of doing this. You might put on some background music and ask people to come forward to share what God has put on their heart. Or you could put a flip chart up and ask people to write on it. I did this once in a prayer meeting in Salisbury. I put four flip charts up around the room and then asked people to wait on the presence of God. We asked God to give us strategic revelation about how we could begin to touch the youth of that city. Then I asked people to go and write down what God gave them on the boards, without looking at what other people had written. After ten minutes we collected the different boards and just read out what had been written, with the purpose of seeing whether any themes were emerging.

The results were amazing. The same themes came out on all the boards, even with the same Scriptures quoted more than once. In fact, the pastors took the paper from these flip charts at the end of the evening, called all their leaders together, and worked on the basis of this revelation over the next year to see those things brought to fruition. For instance, a number of people had referred to working with the youth at a particular venue in the town; it was on each of the four charts. People had connected with something that was clearly on God's heart.

It is good to encourage newer Christians to share what revelation they have received, too. Sometimes we have the attitude that only mature believers hear worthwhile things from God, but God loves to speak out of the mouths of babes! It might not sound perfect, but that does not matter. Hear the spirit of what is being said and weave it in, but encourage their revelation to come.

6. Be teachable

I learned to pray in Africa and so although I am a white English woman, culturally I pray quite differently from many Westerners. When I pray, I love to walk and talk; I am loud and love to declare and proclaim. But I have had to learn to adjust my style and language of prayer when praying with other denominations and nations. In Norway, for instance, people had to take me aside and say to me, "Sorry, but we just can't handle it when you pray like that! Please don't do it because it really irritates the people." Should we adapt our style of prayer just to keep people happy? Yes, I believe we can learn to be sensitive to those we are praying with and not alienate them. You have to be teachable and allow others to influence the way in which you pray. But as you build a relationship of trust and friendship, you can have the joy of influencing their prayer life and teaching them a new expression of prayer.

Proverbs 9:8 says, "Rebuke a wise man and he will love you." Often I will say to people, "I want to come and talk to you about something because I love you!" We need to be able to be that open with one another, to be able to hear someone else's point of view and receive godly direction, as well as gently pointing out things to them. In a prayer meeting, just one or two unteachable people who will not adjust or yield to the atmosphere of a meeting can completely ruin it. Prayer leaders need to face these disruptive situations and deal with them for the good of the whole group, lovingly addressing anyone who is behaving like a maverick, and gently speaking to those who are not tuned in to what the Holy Spirit is doing and are maybe constantly praying about their own agenda or pet cause.

We need to lovingly confront one another when this happens, and we need to be teachable. For too long the prayer meeting has been the meeting where anything goes. We need to deal with the attitude that often sounds like a veiled threat— "But God has said to me!"—and be humble and listen to others. People think they can vent all manner of frustrations and private agendas. No! You need to remain open and teachable and respect the leadership that has been set for the prayer meeting.

7. Be sensitive

In the place of corporate prayer we need to be sensitive to the Holy Spirit, and also to those around us. Prayer leaders need to become skilled at tuning in to where the Holy Spirit is leading the meeting and then keep the prayer on topic. For this illustration, liken the prayer meeting to learning to play tennis. When a child first learns to play, he or she often starts by hitting the ball against a wall. In that situation you can just pick up the ball and hit it where you like because every ball on the court is your ball. But once you begin to play tennis with someone else across a net, the ball will land in unexpected places and completely different skills are needed to have a successful game. In the prayer meeting the topic of prayer is like the ball. When we pray on our own we control the topic of prayer, but this changes once we are in a prayer meeting. Here we need the skill of a good prayer leader to get the "ball" wherever it lands and keep it in play. Just as there is nothing more frustrating than when you serve and the person on the other side of the net hits the ball with all his or her might and it goes into orbit, so it is counter-productive when people pray their prayers into some unreal realm instead of keeping the topic "in play."

Prayer leaders, therefore, need to be prepared to gently bring things back on track, and rescue errant "balls" that fly off somewhere strange! Many a prayer meeting would have been saved if the leader had the courage to bring the topic of prayer back in line.

More pointers for corporate prayer meetings

The following are further pointers regarding skills we all need to learn for our corporate prayer meetings. They are practical points that should help you improve your prayer communication and prevent you from getting off track.

▶ *Do not constantly change subjects in the middle of your prayers*

Keep both to the subject and the focus of the meeting. Otherwise, it is a huge frustration for people who have come to the meeting in response to a request to pray about a certain issue. If people keep losing focus, then prayer leaders need to be prepared to bring them back on track. If there are several subjects, then ensure that people have prayed for a particular theme before it is changed.

▶ *Do not mumble*

Other people want to hear and agree with your prayers, so they must be able to understand you! Prayer leaders need to encourage people to speak up, or perhaps hand around the microphone in larger gatherings. When you pray it is important to give a loud and clear "amen" at the end so that others know they can now pray. Is it "religious" to insist on that? No, it just makes it easier for other people to identify when you have finished. Leaders can ask people to do this with good humor at the beginning of a meeting.

▶ *If you do not agree, say so, but not publicly*

This is more specifically for prayer triplets. If you do not agree with what someone has prayed, it is better to stop and discuss it than to sit on it and let the issue fester. But in open prayer meetings, please *do not* begin to correct another person's prayers by praying something corrective yourself! I have literally witnessed prayer "competitions" in prayer meetings: "Of course, Lord, we know that what has just been prayed is wrong and what you want to do is . . . " Prayer leaders need to make sure that this kind of thing does not happen in their meetings. If necessary, say, "Excuse me, we are not going to do that here." People need to feel secure that under our prayer leadership they are safe.

▶ *Do not try to communicate a prayer need to the rest of the group through your prayers*

Often someone will try to let a prayer need be known to the group by telling others about it in his or her prayer. It causes people to pray things like: "Oh, Lord, you know how I bumped into my neighbor today while she was out walking her dog and she said this to me. . . . " We have a crazy, unwritten rule in church prayer meetings that once we begin praying, we cannot stop to give information on a prayer need. But it is much better to stop and say, "Can we just pray for my neighbor?" Give permission to your group to stop and share when necessary and then you can all pray about that need.

▶ *Do not be an accuser of the brethren*

I am very strict on this. You must not point the finger at other people in prayer, no matter how subtly you disguise it. You

must never use the context of prayer to communicate something about a person to the rest of the group. We need to pray
with love and genuine compassion for our fellow believers
without judging or criticizing them. God is not interested in
your telling Him about everybody else's faults! This is true even
in a small setting like the prayer triplet. Here you must not fall
into the trap of praying accusatory prayers. We need to be
broken over our own sin, not sitting in judgment of other
people's.

▶ *Guard your heart*

We need to guard our hearts as God begins to take us into His
confidence (I have mentioned this in the section on discernment in chapter 3). Make sure that if God shows you something
you use the information wisely. Occasionally I have been in
meetings where people have spoken out prophetically and the
information they shared was quite sensitive. I have usually
taken people to one side and gently asked them if they realized
the impact of what they were sharing. Be discreet. Keep
information to yourself and pray about what God would have
you do with it before releasing it.

▶ *Do not be afraid of silence*

Make sure that everyone in your prayer group/prayer meeting
feels comfortable and understands the times of silence in
prayer. In that time, teach the group how to just wait. It may
be that in the silence God gives a picture or a word to someone.
It is okay for people to be still and just sit in God's presence.

▶ *Follow the leading of the Spirit*

Do organize your meetings, do have a structure and an idea of
where you are going, but remember you do not have to stick to
it like glue. Sometimes, as you may have discovered, the Holy

Spirit does not seem to follow your agenda! You may have ten points to pray about and even the notes to go with them, but as you put them up, you just know the Holy Spirit is prompting you to spend most of your time focusing on point number 7. You may pray all evening for that one point and never get to the others—but that is okay. In terms of executing your prayer list it looks like a disaster, but no, you have prayed the will of God. So why plan at all, you may ask? You plan because it prepares your heart. It takes me just as long to prepare for a prayer meeting as it does to preach the Word, sometimes even longer, because in a prayer meeting you have to communicate and impart a burden to pray *without* preaching! As you prepare, it is a good idea to ask God to give you pictures or illustrations that will quickly demonstrate His heartcry for that issue and then give that to the people when encouraging them to pray.

I believe with all my heart that now is the time to let the sound of prayer from every nation, generation and denomination fill our churches again. This should be an exciting, fulfilling adventure where the army of ordinary people begins to connect with the extraordinary heart of God and the community. I have been thrilled to watch, over the last ten years, the Church beginning to become a house of prayer again. This is so exciting—now is a time to pray and enjoy it!

Tears: The Liquid Prayer of Power

In my church prayer room we had an inflatable globe. I was walking through this room one day and saw the globe and picked it up. As I did, God spoke to me and said, "My burden is easy and light. With Me you can carry the whole world in your hands and heart!" I knew then that it was possible to carry a whole nation in prayer, and yet for that burden to seem easy and light to bear if God had ordained it. When we think of carrying our neighbors or our communities in prayer, we can tend to be overwhelmed by the seeming enormity of the task. Yet when God puts His burden upon us, it is easy and light.

Can an ordinary person really carry a whole nation in prayer? You would think this would be difficult, as the burden would be too heavy. But God helps you carry it. He can put the whole world in your hands—like holding a light, inflatable globe—and it will not be too much to bear. It is not going to break you because He will *grace you* to carry it.

But how does one pray for a nation? The simple answer: You have to let the Holy Spirit show you what God feels for that nation. You might even pray, "Put this nation in my hands, Lord." You do not have to try to work up the enthusiasm to pray yourself because God is able supernaturally to place a nation in your hand, in your heart, so that praying for it will be easy.

I have called this chapter "Tears: The Liquid Prayer of Power" because what will enable you to pray will be your ability to hear the heartcry of God for the lost, for your community, for nations. Someone once said, "The heart of the matter is the matter of the heart." This is true in the place of prayer: You will be drawn to a place where a desperation to pray for the harvest will grip your heart; and when the Holy Spirit touches your heart this deeply, inevitably there will be tears.

In chapter 3 we looked at how God begins to deal with our attitudes and softens our hearts with compassion as we go deeper with Him. We looked at the Scripture in Ezekiel 11:19 that says,

> "I will give them an undivided heart and put a new spirit in them; I will remove from them their heart of stone and give them a heart of flesh."

The wonderful thing about God is that He can do heart surgery on us. He can operate on the stony, hardened areas of our heart and replace them with a heart of flesh. An obvious difference between stone and flesh is that stone feels nothing, but flesh is sensitive; it feels and responds. Therefore, we have to make a decision if we want to be intercessors: Are we going to allow God to make us vulnerable by softening our hearts? Are you willing to allow God to operate on your heart so that you really feel for people and are moved by compassion? It is so much easier to have a heart of stone! That way you do not get hurt and you do not feel the pain of others. Yet, if we really want to connect with the Father's heart and be truly intimate with Him, we cannot avoid feeling what He feels, and our hearts must become a place where He can put His heartcry for the world within us. We have to allow ourselves to become vulnerable enough to weep with those who are weeping—to be touched by the pain of others.

Many of us have allowed a stony heart to develop as a protection against pain. We do not want to get hurt. But remember how Jesus was in Luke 19:41 where we read,

> As he [Jesus] approached Jerusalem and saw the city, he wept over it.

Jesus saw beyond the hustle and bustle of city life and was moved with incredible compassion for the lost and hopeless people the city contained. When is the last time you walked the streets of your city and really "saw" it—not just the bricks and mortar, but behind the façade, you felt the pain of the inhabitants and you wept? You saw a single mother pushing a stroller, saw her loneliness, her desperation, and you wept for her as you felt her dissatisfaction with life. You saw a smart businessman with his nice suit and briefcase, looking every bit the top executive; yet behind that façade was a terrible vacuum and you wept for him. When was the last time you saw the homeless on the street, saw their destitution, and you walked away and wept? When was the last time you saw the kids coming out of school, walking down the hill, their eyes so vacant, their language so filthy, and you watched and wept?

Jesus saw His city and He wept. Jesus heard the silent cry of mankind. I once saw a poster in a doctor's office that affected me deeply and I have never forgotten it. It said, "Both a newborn baby and a teenager possess a cry that is deep and loud. However, only one cry can be heard easily, but both need urgent parental attention."

When a newborn baby cries, the need is more obvious. You know the baby needs something and as a parent you go and attend to it. But out in your community is the silent cry of a teenage generation longing for the touch of parental care; longing for a mom or a dad to pick them up and nurture them. Because their cry is an internal one, it is often missed. But the heart of the Father does not miss their cry. And beyond our teenagers we have a generation crying out in need. Can you hear the silent distress of your community?

I believe that in these days God wants to seriously damage our comfort zones and our sense of complacency. We have tended to shield ourselves from all that is going on around us in society, but our spirits need to be awakened to the cries of our communities and cities. We need to pray and let God get at our hearts! I call this type of prayer *birthing* or *travailing* prayer. It is prayer that allows God to get deep into our hearts and reveal to us His pain and longing for people. As He begins to reveal His heart to us, so we begin to carry the pain and distress of those around us and begin to pray for them. As this revelation touches our lives, the Spirit of God births something new in us.

How devastated are you?

If I may, I want to irritate you with some uncomfortable questions. I want to lovingly challenge you to take a look at your heart and examine it. I want to ask: How "devastated" are you by what God has revealed to you? It is not a particularly attractive word or concept and yet the Bible talks about being "ruined" when we encounter the Person of God. Coming face-to-face with almighty God is an experience that ruins and devastates us. Similarly, I believe that in this season God wants to step into our nice, organized, nine-to-five existences and ruin us with a vision of the pain of our communities and the vast harvest field that awaits us. I believe that God is challenging us to examine how devastated we are regarding three critical areas: our sin, our barrenness and our powerlessness.

1. Does sin devastate you?

Isaiah 6:5 says,

> "Woe to me!" I cried. "I am ruined [devastated]! For I am a man
> of unclean lips, and I live among a people of unclean lips, and
> my eyes have seen the King, the LORD Almighty."

If we are going to be a people who carry compassion and a soft
heart toward others, we need to be a people who carry a right
sense of sin. We need to have a horror and a devastation
regarding our sin. We need to carry with us an awareness of
the cross of Jesus, of what He did for us on the cross, that
our sins have been forgiven. In a right sense we need to carry
the truth that we are all sinners, doomed but for the grace of
God. If we truly realized how God has delivered us from sin, we
would have a much greater sense of urgency to rescue others
from their sin.

When this prophet Isaiah stands in the presence of God, the
first revelation he gets is not of the people's sin, but of his own
sin, of who he is, but for the grace of God. He stands before
God and says, "Oh, God, I'm a sinner!" Then he realizes he is
one among a whole generation of sinners. First his own sin
devastates him, and then he is devastated by the sin in the lives
of the people around him. Now he realizes that his eyes have
seen the King, the one pure, spotless, wonderful Lamb of God
who is able to deliver all people from their sin. He knows that
his sinful generation needs God and so he is prepared to go and
be used by God to reach each of them.

Reading further in Isaiah, we see that the word of the Lord
comes to Isaiah and challenges him. First the angel of the
Lord comes to him and touches his mouth saying, "See . . . your
guilt is taken away and your sin atoned for" (verse 7), and then
the challenge comes:

Then I heard the voice of the Lord saying, "Whom shall I send?
And who will go for us?"
And I said, "Here am I. Send me!"

Isaiah 6:8

If we are going to be used by God, to be "sent" as Isaiah was, to reach our communities, we need to be prepared to cry many tears. I believe God is going to put that heart of compassion in us concerning the sin of our cities; we are going to weep for the people's sin just as Isaiah did.

In Hebrews 1:9 it is written about Jesus that He, "loved righteousness and hated wickedness." Jesus loved righteousness, but equally He *hated* wickedness. So often we love righteousness but we do not have an equivalent deep hatred of wickedness. I want to ask you: Do you hate sin and what it is doing in your community? Do you hate the way that sin grips people's lives and ruins them? We have to begin to hate sin with a passion. We need to be able to hate the sin in our lives and hate the sin in the community, because it is robbing people.

Having a right understanding of what sin does in the lives of people is one thing that will drive us to our knees in prayer. The power of sin is gripping our cities. A hatred of sin needs to grip our lives and humble us. It needs to provoke more than just repentance in us; it needs to put a heartcry in the Church: "Oh, God, save our cities!" God wants some liquid prayer.

2. Does barrenness devastate you?

I am writing more about this in my second book, *Supernatural Breakthrough—the Heartcry for Change*, but I want to touch on it here. I believe one of the main things the Holy Spirit is bringing to the attention of Christians in the West today is our utter spiritual barrenness. Although there are pockets of good things happening in our nations, mostly we do not see the power of

God poured out. We have not seen the breakthrough into signs, miracles and wonders that we need to see if revival is to come to our land. We have become barren but have hidden our condition with many excuses!

The story of Hannah in 1 Samuel 1 describes her desperation to break the curse of barrenness from her life and have a child. Here we discover that Hannah was one of two wives to her husband, Elkanah. She had a good, intimate relationship with her husband and he clearly loved her deeply. She was blessed, she had intimacy, but she had no children.

In the past I have often taught on the subject of seeking intimacy with God through prayer, but now I have come to the conclusion that even intimacy on its own is not enough! It will not satisfy forever. All intimacy should lead to fruitfulness. We are made to be fruitful and satisfied. Hannah had a good, intimate relationship with her husband and Elkanah swore his undying love for her. In our Christian lives, many of us can draw a parallel to Hannah's relationship with her husband. We have known wonderful intimacy with the Father and we have been deeply touched and blessed. But there is more.

No doubt Hannah enjoyed and appreciated her relationship with Elkanah, but there was still something missing. She longed to be fruitful. Eventually Hannah grew so desperate that she cried out to God and refused to let go until He blessed her with a child, but before she reached that place her love rival, Elkanah's other wife, Peninnah, sorely provoked her. Peninnah would deliberately mock and provoke Hannah, constantly reminding her that in spite of all her blessing she had borne no fruit. Peninnah, of course, had. "You may have intimacy, but actually you are barren," was the clear message.

In these days God is allowing the Church to be provoked in the same way. He is sending "Peninnahs" to stir us up, to help us realize we need to move beyond the intimacy and blessing;

this is the time for fruitfulness. The Peninnahs sometimes come in the form of people who mock the Church and say to us, "If your God is so powerful, why can't He heal cancer?"; "If your God is so powerful, why can't He save my marriage?" Such statements might offend us, but God allows these things to provoke us to realize our barrenness.

It is time for the Church to move beyond making excuses as to why we do not see God's power poured out, and like Hannah, it is time for us to reach a place of desperation. This final provocation pushed Hannah to such a level of desperation in the place of prayer that she threw herself before God and refused to leave the altar until He heard her. She would not stop crying out to God, "Oh, God, intimacy is no longer enough— I've got to have fruitfulness!" In 1 Samuel 1:8 we even see Elkanah pleading with Hannah not to be so desperate:

> "Hannah, why are you weeping? Why don't you eat? Why are you downhearted? Don't I mean more to you than ten sons?"

The Bible records no response from Hannah. The implication of her silence is, "No!"

Hannah became so anguished, so distressed, that the people around her thought she had completely lost it, but something was being birthed in Hannah in that season of tears. Her barrenness was going to be broken; she was going to give birth to the son of promise, which was her destiny, her calling, but it took desperation to get to that place.

I believe God is beginning to challenge the Church over our laziness and complacency. We have given too many excuses. We know God's presence, the Holy Spirit, moves in our meetings … but the Holy Spirit is asking us the question, "Where is the fruitfulness?" This intimacy has to lead to fruitfulness. Hannah's barrenness had lasted for years. Year after year she had denied the cry for life within her body so that, in the end, God had to use Peninnah to provoke her to reach out and grasp her destiny. Similarly, the Church was born to demonstrate the power of God with signs and wonders. For too long we have continued our programs with many words but little power, and God now provokes us and challenges our barrenness. But once we are truly desperate, then we will begin to see the breakthrough that will touch nations.

3. Does powerlessness devastate you?

In the Western Church we need to embrace this desperation and confess to God that we are barren. Compared to our brothers and sisters in Christ in other parts of the world, we are naked, poor, wretched and blind. As a result I believe God wants to take us into a season of tears where He strips away all our falsehood and puts a desperation on us—not depression or self-pity, but divine desperation. He wants to reawaken in us the cry of destiny we have smothered with good excuses. We are powerless, but we know that our God is not. We must throw off all complacency and pray that God will do something in us.

Remember Jesus' words in Matthew 10:7:

> "As you go, preach this message: 'The kingdom of heaven is near.'"

How did Jesus preach the message of the Kingdom? How does He expect us to go? He gives the answer in the following verse:

> "Heal the sick, raise the dead, cleanse those who have leprosy, drive out demons. Freely you have received, freely give."
>
> Matthew 10:8

Did Jesus say, "Except for the Western world, of course, where different rules apply"? No! It does not say heal the sick except in countries where they have excellent government or private healthcare. Jesus' words reveal that signs and wonders are an explicit demonstration that the Kingdom of God is at hand. It is obvious where the Kingdom of heaven touches the earth because there is the power to heal cancer, to raise the dead, to deliver people from demonic fear and oppression.

The words of the prophet Joel strike home in our hearts in these days:

> Blow the trumpet in Zion,
>> declare a holy fast,
>> call a sacred assembly.
> Gather the people,
>> consecrate the assembly;
> bring together the elders,
>> gather the children,
>> those nursing at the breast.
> Let the bridegroom leave his room
>> and the bride her chamber.
> Let the priests, who minister before the LORD,
>> weep between the temple porch and the altar.
> Let them say, "Spare your people, O LORD.
>> Do not make your inheritance an object of scorn,
>> a byword among the nations.
> Why should they say among the peoples,
>> 'Where is their God?'"

> Joel 2:15–17

"Where is your God?" people often protest. Personally I am weary of that cry in Europe, America and Canada. I long for them to say, "I know your God!" But they have still got every reason to say, "Where is their God?" They say it because they often cannot see any evidence of God in their community or in the Church. This is why, as Joel exhorts, we need to blow the distress call and gather the Church together. Now is a gathering time—a time to come together in a time of crisis and emergency. We need to gather together and cry out to God, "Spare the nations, O God. Help us!"

Joel says, "Let us weep before the altar." We need to weep because there are nations going to hell. We need to cry out, "God have mercy on us!" We need God to strip away every area of our pride and arrogance, and fall upon Him. We need to cry tears of repentance and ask God to change our hearts to pray for others, and to empower us in our weakness.

Like the great Welsh revivalist Evan Roberts, we need to pray, "Lord, bend us! Lord, break us!" It does not sound like a very elegant prayer, but it is a desperate prayer from deep within—a prayer of alignment between heaven and earth.

When God begins to grip us with that sense of urgency and desperation, we will feel His heartbeat and it will make us weep. He will open our ears to the cries of the world, to His heartcry, and we will begin to echo the heartbeat of God into our communities.

Learning God's cry for others

I believe we are in a season of weeping with warfare. We cannot afford to have the triumphalistic "just watch us, here we come" attitude that some seem to express. Successful spiritual warfare is born out of brokenness. It comes from a heart that says, "God we really need You or we are finished."

Some verses from Lamentations 2 aptly describe what our attitude should be like in this season:

> The hearts of the people
> cry out to the Lord.

O wall of the Daughter of Zion,
  let your tears flow like a river
  day and night;
give yourself no relief,
  your eyes no rest.

Arise, cry out in the night,
  as the watches of the night begin;
pour out your heart like water
  in the presence of the Lord.
Lift up your hands to him
  for the lives of your children,
who faint from hunger
  at the head of every street.

Lamentations 2:18–19, emphasis added

I was in a meeting recently where the people were singing, "Let your river flow." We have many romantic ideas about the river of God only being a river of blessing, but I believe one of the expressions of this river that God wants to flow in the Church is the river of tears.

We need to learn to cry out to God for the lives of others: our cities, towns, communities, neighbors and children. In the West we do not think we need to pray for our children as this verse suggests. Our children are not hungry like many African children are. But if it were possible to see the spiritual and emotional well-being of a child, as it is the physical well-being, then the majority of Western children would appear more emaciated and malnourished than those we have seen from the Sudan on our TV screens. Emotionally and spiritually, our children are starving! Take some time to look into the eyes of the children on your streets. So many of them are filled with fear and torment. What is the remedy for fear? Love. We need to love those kids with God's love because they are the next generation of mothers and fathers.

This season of weeping and tears is not just a woman's thing. The Holy Spirit can also provoke men to cry and weep. In Jeremiah 30:6–7 we read,

> "Ask and see:
>   Can a man bear children?
> Then why do I see every strong man
>   with his hands on his stomach like
>   a woman in labor,
>   every face turned deathly pale?
> How awful that day will be!
>   None will be like it.
> It will be a time of trouble for Jacob,
>   but he will be saved out of it."

Watch out, men, you are about to get pregnant! The Scripture goes on to foretell a time when the yokes will be broken off people's necks and a time of deliverance will come. I believe a critical element in bringing the Church into a season of breakthrough is when the men begin to cry out, to feel that compassion and carry the burden of desperation for their nation. This is why God is beginning to grip many men in the place of prayer.

God is calling men and women to work together, shoulder to shoulder, because our nations are in a season of pain and trouble. Women are being called to be warriors and men are being called to weep. We have got to break the cultural code that says, "Real men don't cry." What rubbish! God wants men to be connected with their emotions again, not to have their emotions put in a box and disconnected from their manhood. God wants to reconnect men with their emotions, because we need fathers with compassion in our communities.

Part of connecting with God's heartcry for our communities is learning how to carry a burden for someone else in prayer. Galatians 6:2 says,

> Carry each other's burdens, and in this way you will fulfill the law of Christ.

The Greek word for "burdens" is *baros* and literally means "a weighty, heavy load." That is why sometimes in the presence of God you can feel as though a great weight is upon you. This happens when God allows you to feel the *baros*, the burden, the weighty sense of a need. It is a spiritual burden.

God wants you to carry such a burden for your community, your city. Just like a pregnant woman carrying her child, it is often not comfortable. You cannot just put the burden down at your convenience; you have to wait for the birth. God is going to allow those weighty things to rest on our spirits. He is looking for a Church that will come and carry the community burdens in the place of prayer.

Cooperating with burdens

We have looked prophetically at what I believe the Holy Spirit is stirring in the Church at present. I could sum it all up by saying that God wants us to *take responsibility*. He wants us to be responsible in prayer for the lives of those around us and to carry specific burdens as He gives them to us. For the remainder of this chapter, I want to give some practical advice on how to recognize and handle the different types of spiritual burden that the Lord might want us to bear. Sometimes the Lord will ask us to pray a simple one-liner prayer for another person. At other times He will ask us to pray for a specific aspect of community life for a longer period of time. There are different ways of cooperating with these burdens and praying through them. I trust you will find this helpful as you grow in your prayer life.

Cooperating with different types of burden

1. Immediate or impulse burdens

Some burdens come upon your spirit instantaneously and you can immediately recognize when this happens. Once you have prayed about the matter, whatever it might be, the burden lifts very quickly. We have all read in books about intercessors that are woken by the Lord in the middle of the night and have a sense of urgency to pray for a missionary or some nation. Maybe they do not even know what they are praying for, and then suddenly the burden lifts. Later, perhaps the next day or next week, they receive a phone call or a letter that explains why God wanted them to pray at that specific time. They realize that the burden they cooperated with was actually protecting or helping someone in a time of emergency.

Often we do not know why such burdens come. They are like the emergency alarm of the Holy Spirit, calling us into action. He is calling our emergency number and saying, "Wake up!" When you say, "God, here am I, use me," guess what? He believes you! So when God is looking into the community and sees a problem, He calls your number. God is always looking for someone who will stand in the gap and pray. The Holy Spirit brings us the prayer requests of heaven and when that happens it requires priority attention.

I recall one such occasion when Gordon and I were pastoring a church in Watford, North London. It happened while I was ironing clothes. We had been pastoring the church for a little while and during that time a woman came to us, whom I will call Rebecca (not her real name), who had been involved in drugs and alcohol and had quite a tragic background. Gordon and another lady in the church had been working with her and had really seen her get delivered. This day I was doing my ironing when the phone rang and Rebecca was on the other end.

"Could you help me?" she asked.

"Sure," I said. "What would you like me to do?"

Then she asked me if I would meet her daughter off the school bus later that day. "No problem," I said. "What time will you come and collect her?" Rebecca asked me if I would not mind just holding on to her until she arrived as she was not sure yet what time it would be. I said that was fine and we hung up.

As I put the phone down, the Holy Spirit spoke to me clearly: "She's going to try to commit suicide." There was no reason from the phone call to suspect she would do that, but I began to pray. I tried to phone Gordon at the office to discuss it with him, but the line was continually busy. Then the Holy Spirit said to me, "Call an ambulance." *Oh no*, I thought, *how can I call an ambulance when nothing has happened?* But I felt that sense of urgency from the Holy Spirit, that spiritual alarm going off, so in the end I called the emergency services and told them, "I believe a lady I know has tried to commit suicide. This is the address; please, can you go there?" They asked if I would meet them at her house, but I had no transportation.

As soon as finished calling emergency services, I managed to get straight through to the office and told Gordon I had ordered an ambulance to go to Rebecca's house because I believed she was going to attempt suicide. "How do you know that?" he asked. "Because the Holy Spirit spoke to me," I replied.

Gordon dashed over there in the car and arrived at the same time as the emergency services. The apartment was locked, so they called the police, who arrived and kicked the door down.

The ambulance crew went in and found Rebecca, who had indeed taken a serious overdose, one which would undoubtedly have killed her. But the ambulance crew managed to save her life by pumping her stomach immediately. They later told us that if they had attended to her even five minutes later, she would have suffered serious liver and kidney damage. Any later than that and she would have been dead.

Looking back, we realized that the Holy Spirit had prompted me to call an ambulance *before* she had actually taken the overdose. The Holy Spirit knew. Today, God is using this precious woman. She is a wonderful worship leader and God has His hand on her life. The enemy knew that she was going to be a weapon in the hands of God and tried to terminate her, but God's purposes always prevail.

The fact is, God speaks to us. It is not always dramatic, but we need to learn to be responsive to His voice and learn to trust and respect the direction of the Holy Spirit. There have also been times when God spoke to me and I let it slip. Later, when I thought about it, I regretted not doing something about it at the time. We need to respond to that burden because we just do not see what the Holy Spirit can see.

We need to realize that the length of time a burden rests on you is not directly related to the significance of the issue. What I mean by that is, it does not matter how long you pray about a matter—whether it is three hours or three minutes—what matters is getting the job done. I gave birth to two children; one birth took thirty-seven minutes and the other just seven minutes. (My apologies to all the ladies reading this who worked harder!) The fact that these times were short did not mean I did not really give birth; the important thing was that I got the job done and delivered my babies. That is all that mattered at the time. One birth was not more significant than the other because one was longer! Similarly, prayer is about cooperating with the

Holy Spirit to get the job done. Even if that burden is only there for a short time, work with it until it lifts.

Once you have received a burden like this from the Lord, what do you do?

▶ *Begin to worship and pray in the Spirit*
Start by focusing on God and asking Him to direct you. Use your prayer language. Perhaps put some worship music on. Often you will not know what the burden is about. Sometimes you do know, but at other times you just "feel" it.

▶ *Find a place to pray and give the burden priority*
If it happens in the middle of the night, get out of bed and go somewhere else in the house where you can pray and not disturb anyone. If it happens during the day, stop what you are doing and go find a quiet place to pray. Postpone anything else you were going to do until you finish the job at hand. No woman turns up at the hospital to give birth and says, "Can we get this done quickly? I've got a hair appointment in 45 minutes!" If she did, the midwife would undoubtedly say, "Excuse me, but you're here till the job is done!" The moment of giving birth eclipses all other priorities. It is the same with Holy Spirit-inspired burdens of prayer.

▶ *Labor in prayer and keep focused with an attitude of compassion*

▶ *Wait for the burden to lift*
What do I mean by this? Well, eventually the atmosphere just changes. The burden comes and when it has been dealt with, it goes. Once you feel it lift, then just let the burden go. There is nothing more fatiguing than trying to continue to pray for an issue when the burden has lifted. Sometimes you will not know

what the burden was about. Other times you will find out later. God often graciously reveals to us what He has asked us to intercede for because He loves sharing the secrets of heaven with us.

2. Long-term burdens

Then there are long-term burdens. Many of us can identify with this type of burden more readily. It is when God puts something on your heart to pray for over a long period of time. For instance, your city, your community, a certain sphere of society like business people, perhaps, or young people. You know if God has put this burden on you because it is something you come back to again and again. If someone mentions the subject to you, it immediately triggers something in you; you can feel the burden being stirred up. Maybe your long-term burden is the salvation of someone—your father or mother, your children, and so on. Whenever they are mentioned, you feel the burden to pray come upon you. You know it is part of your responsibility in the place of prayer.

Anyone who has carried a burden in prayer for a long time will know that it is easy to wonder if your prayers are having any effect. It is easy to ask, "What is all this prayer actually achieving?" Often we feel like Elijah in 1 Kings 18 when he was praying for rain to come. Elijah was crouched down on Mount Carmel with his head between his knees (see verses 42–45). The Eastern world knows this as the classic birthing position. Here was a man in the birthing position, desperately seeking a breakthrough for his nation. Every time Elijah prayed, he would sense a change and would lift up his head to see if he had the full breakthrough yet. Had it begun to rain?

Do you think Elijah kept lifting his head up because he was in doubt? No. He was a mature prophet. He knew God. He could sense in the spirit when God was doing something. So he put his head down, prayed once, and lifted his head up because he sensed that something had shifted in the spirit. He sent his servant to find out if anything had happened yet. Nothing had visibly changed, so he put his head down and prayed again. How many times did he have to do this? Seven times! In biblical terms seven represents the fullness of time, the perfect time, the completed time. This is what we have to do with our long-term prayer burdens: We put our head down and pray and after a time we look up to see if anything has changed. If it has not, we put our head down again and carry on praying. We have to go back to work to birth that burden of prayer yet again.

As we pray, God is doing something in the spiritual realm, which we cannot yet see in the natural. Even though we cannot see any change yet, we still must persevere in prayer.

At one time, Gordon's brother Brian was part of a cult. One of the sad things for Gordon was that he had converted his brother into this cult when he was just fifteen years old. Gordon then got born again in college, but Brian stayed in this movement. You can imagine that Gordon had a burden to see his brother get saved. He prayed for him consistently but still that journey took over thirty years to complete. Now Brian knows Jesus and is working in Jerusalem.

A while ago God spoke to me from Isaiah 62:10 and showed me what is happening in the spiritual realm as we walk these long-term prayer journeys:

> Pass through, pass through the gates!
> Prepare the way for the people.
> Build up, build up the highway!
> Remove the stones.
> Raise a banner for the nations.

Intercession is about standing in the gap for others. When you pray you are the gap-filler, bridging the void between a person or situation and God. Your Father in heaven wants you to reach out and be the bridge toward those people that He wants to reach. He reaches out and touches you, and you have to stand in the gap between God and that person, and reach out to them to make the connection between that person, you and the Father.

To do this you need to "pass through the gates" of the enemy; in other words, in prayer you storm the opposition that has been built up around that person's life, because you have a mandate to prepare the way for that person to come to God. In prayer we remove stones, obstructions, rubble, anything that hinders the path between that person and the Lord, so that the banner of victory can be declared over that situation.

While Gordon cried out for his brother and labored for him in the place of prayer, he was building a highway for his brother to come to know the Lord. Something was shifting in the spirit, so that eventually the connection between heaven and earth was made. Elijah prayed seven times. We often get to the point where we have prayed three, four, five, even six times, and at that point we give up because we feel we have done it for so long. The message is: Do not give up! Even though you may have carried your prayer burden for a very long time, there will come a perfect day when you will see the breakthrough.

Gordon prayed for his brother for 32 years, but eventually the day came for his prayers to be answered. I remember the evening clearly. There was a prayer meeting at church. It was not a particularly great meeting and I was actually clock-watching, thinking, *When can we stop and go home?* I suggested people form small groups and pray especially for any family member who was not yet saved. I thought, *Maybe that will take fifteen minutes, then we can all go home.* After the meeting I asked Gordon whom he had prayed for. "Brian," he said. "I felt God tell me to pray for Brian, too," I said. We walked into the house that night and the answering machine's light was flashing.

Gordon played the message: "Gordon, it's Brian here. I really need to talk to you. Can we get together sometime soon?" Gordon called him and went down to see him. To cut a long story short, the night when Gordon met with his brother, the connection between heaven and earth was made.

So after 32 years of carrying the burden and laboring in the place of prayer, there came a day when the time was right for fulfillment, and it was worth the wait. To those of you who are also carrying long-term burdens: The time of fulfillment will come and it is going to be worth it. Just like when you finally hold the baby after the hard work of labor and you quickly forget the pain because you are overwhelmed with the new gift of life, so it is with the joy of answered prayer. The years of hardship and struggle all melt away as you look at the answer to your prayers and you know *every* tear was worth it. You can now touch and handle your dreams—it is mission accomplished!

God is bringing us into a season of fruitfulness. The barren land is going to be turned and we are going to repossess our cities. But we have to be a people with a heartcry of desperation, ready to carry the burden, prepared to touch a needy world.

Spiritual Warfare for the Ordinary Person

Spiritual warfare—just this term can cause controversy and immediate confusion. Since this is such a huge subject and there are so many specialist books, CDs, manuals and DVDs on spiritual warfare available today, I am not going to attempt to cover the subject thoroughly in a single chapter of a book on general prayer. But I do want to concentrate on the areas of spiritual warfare that I believe are vital for any prayer warrior. In this chapter I want to explain spiritual warfare in simple terms that ordinary people can grasp. Instead of viewing spiritual warfare as a specialist activity carried out by experts, I want to bring it back from the complicated realms and answer some basic questions:

- What spiritual warfare do I face day to day?
- How does spiritual warfare affect my life and what do I have to do about it?
- Is this a specialist activity for certain occasions only or do I have to be more involved?

When the term *spiritual warfare* is mentioned, many people immediately have a mental picture that is based more on the books by Frank Peretti or horror movies than the Bible. They are tempted to feel that demonic forces now surround us, and so our prayers are like rifles, shooting these demons out of the sky or from under the bed! But what is the right picture of spiritual warfare?

There are two pictures that the Holy Spirit gives us of the Church throughout the Bible and I believe these are helpful to our understanding of spiritual warfare. The first is the picture of a *family*. We learn that God is our Father and we are His children; we are all brothers and sisters in Christ; we have family relationships. The other picture is that of an *army*, where the Lord is our Commander, the Lord of Hosts. Remember when an angel confronted Joshua at the time of the fall of Jericho? As he approached the city, Joshua saw a "man" with a drawn sword and asked him if he was on his side or on his enemies' side. The man replied, "Neither . . . but as commander of the army of the LORD I have now come" (Joshua 5:14).

Throughout the book of Revelation, Jesus is portrayed as our majestic Warrior King on a horse as the time approaches for the great battle of the age. As individual believers we are taught by Paul in the book of Ephesians the need to be clothed in spiritual armor in order to be properly protected as we engage the enemy.

So we are a family, but a family that must also learn to function as an army, because we are at war! Some of us do not like the idea of the Church being at war—we even react to the word *warfare*. We are much more comfortable with the concept of a Church being our safe family environment. But in order to understand the full dimensions of our God and our relationship with Him, we must hold both these two facets of the Church in tension, and, therefore, in our own lives. The word *warfare* is in God's vocabulary! We have to overcome our tendency for passivism and desire for security and see the face of our Warrior King. Although you might not feel much like a warrior when you get up in the morning, you need to allow the Holy Spirit, who is a warrior, to reveal that aspect of His nature to you and let it touch your life.

We need to learn the appropriate times to respond to God as our Father or to God as our Heavenly Commander. There will be times when we need to touch God as our "Daddy," to be intimate, to be lost in worship. Those times will be very personal. But there will also be times when we need relate to God as the Majestic Commander of the Hosts of Heaven. At those times we need to come into His presence with a sense of awe and respect, like a soldier who is reporting for duty; we enter His presence to collect our orders because we want to serve our King and Lord.

I began to understand a little about the military lifestyle and that sense of belonging to an army after marrying my husband, Gordon. His family is a military family. Gordon's father was a colonel and Gordon, when I met him, was a captain in the army. It was interesting to me that in the early days, Gordon tended to relate to his father as "the Colonel" more than he did as just his "dad," although this changed over the years. It was an illustration to me of what is appropriate behavior in the presence of your Commander.

Gordon went to Sandhurst Military Academy. He "passed out" with the award for the most outstanding officer in the Royal Artillery Regiment. At the passing-out parade, the officers walk out in front of their colonel-in-chief. Although this next part did not actually happen, imagine with me for a moment that at Gordon's passing-out parade, the presiding colonel was his father. Think how inappropriate it would have been if on that day Gordon had run up and hugged the colonel in front of all the other officers and exclaimed, "Daddy, isn't it exciting? I won the award!" It would have been totally inappropriate behavior! Instead, you need to honor the serious-ness of the situation and fulfill your duty with appropriate behavior. This occasion calls for the officer to march up to the colonel, accept his award with a dignified salute and say, "Yes, sir. Thank you, sir," and then step back.

I believe there are times when we have become frivolous children in God's presence when actually it is time for battle. The Commander is saying to us, "Come on! Stand up straight, head up, shoulders back. Get ready to march!" but we are still saying, "Daddy, I don't like it! I want to stay here and be with You!" God is saying, "Do it!" but all we want to do is go and play!

I believe God is calling us to be mighty warriors. God wants to train your hands for battle. As you look into your commun-ity, don't you see an enemy that is plundering and stealing? There is a terrorist that prowls our streets, going from home to home, disturbing marriages and wounding families. There should be times when something within you is provoked and you rise up and declare, "No! Enough is enough!" Don't you think your Father in heaven feels that sense of indignation? Jesus hung on the cross. What an act of warfare that was. The whole of hell was laughing, saying, "Ha! We've won." But suddenly, out of the grave, a terrible sound began to rumble and it hit hell first! There was a shout and a declaration, "I have conquered death!" People of God, we are at war!

In Psalm 18:32–39 we read the declaration of David, the worshiping warrior king:

> It is God who arms me with strength
> and makes my way perfect.
> He makes my feet like the feet of a deer;
> he enables me to stand on the heights.
> He trains my hands for battle;
> my arms can bend a bow of bronze.

You give me your shield of victory,
and your right hand sustains me;
you stoop down to make me great.
You broaden the path beneath me,
so that my ankles do not turn.

I pursued my enemies and overtook them;
I did not turn back till they were destroyed.
I crushed them so that they could not rise;
they fell beneath my feet.
You armed me with strength for battle;
you made my adversaries bow at my feet.

It is undeniably militant language. There is no doubt that as Christians we need to have and to demonstrate great compassion in order to reach out to the lost. But I firmly believe that at the same time we need to possess a holy indignation and anger against the devil's schemes. We need to reflect the two faces of Jesus; we need to have both the Lion and the Lamb nature! We need to hate the author of sin and wickedness; we need to hate the evil one and all his ways. I believe that warrior spirit needs to permeate our character.

The wake-up call of the Holy Spirit

I believe that at this time the Holy Spirit is urging the Church to wake up and realize that, whether we like it or not, we are at war. We have been passive for far too long about the things that are happening around us—in our communities, across our nation. We have tended to sit back and say, "It's none of my business." We have become too tolerant and politically correct and not wanted to rock the boat and say *no* to sin. The wake-up call is: It is your business! Whether you want to be involved or not, you are involved because this has to do with the advance of God's Kingdom.

There is a war going on for the control of our nation. There is a wrestling in the spirit between the standards of God and the standards of wickedness. It often looks as though we, the people of God, are losing the battle as the darkness closes in. The battle for sexual purity is raging; there is a battle for the preservation of marriage; there is a battle for simple integrity and truth. In these days, the Church needs to be trained and armed for war in order to win these battles. God wants to wake us up so that we will cry out with David, "God, train my hands for battle! I am weak, but with Your help I can be strong!"

Wartime priorities

During wartime, our priorities in life become very different. When we are at war, certain issues become less important and other decisions critical. Here are five areas that spring to mind.

1. In wartime, suddenly, unity is no longer a problem or an issue

A government can be in complete disarray, split into numerous political factions, each vehemently defending their views, but when war is declared and the nation is under threat, suddenly everyone is pulling together. Look how the events of 9/11 have affected America. They have had a unifying effect and have caused people to close ranks.

Unity is not a problem when you are focused on a known enemy. I believe if the Church became unified in its focus upon its true enemy, the devil, unity between the churches would not be the challenge it currently is. Suddenly our slight theological differences would not seem so important, as we would realize lives are at stake and there is a real enemy in the camp. Yet many are still living under the delusion that we are not at war. We think we are living in peacetime and are playing games while the enemy is busy plundering our cities.

2. In wartime, teamwork and cooperation become vital tools for success

No one person can fight the enemy; it has to be done together. Around the world prophetic people are uttering words such as *shoulder to shoulder* and *networking*. I believe it points to the fact that God wants to build us together. He is unifying believers, not just in our local churches, but across the generation gap, the gender barrier and the denominational lines; He is calling people together from across the nations, too. He is mobilizing His army!

3. In wartime, personal preference no longer counts

In the army you eat what you are told to eat, you wear what you are told to wear, you turn up when you are summoned and you go wherever you are ordered to go. You even live where you are told to live! Think back to the Second World War. Even children in England were taken from their families and relocated in other homes where they would be safe. You had very little say in what was happening because personal preference no longer counted. There was a higher priority.

4. Instant obedience is expected in a time of war

If a soldier is given an order, then he must comply immediately. He cannot say to his commanding officer, "It's not convenient at the moment. Can I do it later?" He would be court-martialed! War is a serious business.

5. Leisure and pleasure are very low priorities in wartime

Leisure and pleasure take a backseat because survival and winning the war are the overriding priorities.

Rousing the warriors

You can easily see why some people are not enthralled by the call to war. It cuts to the heart of everything important in our life and challenges what we are. Joel 2:1 says,

> Blow the trumpet in Zion;
>   sound the alarm on my holy hill.
> Let all who live in the land tremble,
>   for the day of the LORD is coming.
> It is close at hand.

Zion is a picture of the Church and God is blowing His trumpet to assemble the troops for battle. God is trying to catch our attention. He is sounding an alarm. I believe that the Church can marginalize prophetic people because their voice almost sounds like an annoying alarm going off! Alarms are specially designed to irritate and disturb us, so that they will disturb our comfort zones and get us moving! But what is our usual response? "Turn that thing off!"

So, if you have a prophetic gift and God is telling you to awaken the Church, do not get offended if people continually try to silence you! You are irritating them and waking them up just like an alarm clock. Do not worry if they manage to throw your sound out of the window; God will find another "alarm clock" to disturb them, because He is determined to wake up His Church!

So often we seem to have a very romantic idea about revival, but the Bible describes the "day of the Lord" as being a terrifying event. It is a confrontation as light meets darkness, righteousness meets wickedness and something powerful happens. Joel predicted that the whole land would "tremble." Later in Joel we gain a further insight into how the Body of Christ is to be mobilized for battle. Joel 2:15–17 says,

> Blow the trumpet in Zion,
>> declare a holy fast,
>> call a sacred assembly.
> Gather the people,
>> consecrate the assembly;
> bring together the elders,
>> gather the children,
>> those nursing at the breast.
> Let the bridegroom leave his room
>> and the bride her chamber.
> Let the priests, who minister before the LORD,
>> weep between the temple porch and the altar.
> Let them say, "Spare your people, O LORD.
>> Do not make your inheritance an object of scorn,
>> a byword among the nations.
> Why should they say among the peoples,
>> 'Where is their God?' "

God says that we should "declare a holy fast." Wartime is a time of sacrifice. It is going to cost us. During a war the government has to raise taxes in order to meet the cost of the war. War is expensive. As we the Church begin to wage war against some of the demonic powers afflicting our nation, it is going to cost us something. We are going to have to give financially to support ministries that have a mandate from God to fight on the frontline of the battle. We need to make sacrifices so that others can confront these powers and principalities. We need to support prayer ministries and mercy ministries that have compassion on the wounded, the casualties of war that are inevitably incurred. War does have a price.

The Lord also says through His prophet Joel that we should call a sacred assembly. Now is the time for gathering together, and I am not talking about just getting together with other believers at conferences. God is urging believers who share a similar heart and vision to gather together regularly, to respond to the call of the Spirit and come together in unity to pray and see God's will accomplished.

In chapter 3 verses 9–11, Joel writes,

> Proclaim this among the nations:
>> Prepare for war!
> Rouse the warriors!
>> Let all the fighting men draw near and attack.
> Beat your plowshares into swords
>> and your pruning hooks into spears.
> Let the weakling say,
>> "I am strong!"
> Come quickly, all you nations from every side,
>> and assemble there.
> Bring down your warriors, O LORD!

I believe that after the Church has woken up, realized that she is at war and mobilized herself for battle, then we will have something to declare to the nations! This is not a time for the weak to say, "I'm not into this. I'm going home!" Those who feel weak in themselves can be strong in God.

Notice that Joel speaks about fashioning plowshares into swords and pruning hooks into spears. A plowshare was an agricultural tool, something that was used during harvest time for reaping the crops. God is telling us that we need to take our harvesting instruments and change them into weapons. I believe God is saying that we cannot expect to go out and gather in the harvest until we have waged war upon the enemy in the land. How many of us have poured our energy into programs of evangelism and seen a few people saved, but later they seem to drift away and we lose them from the Church? Why does this happen? Because we have not sought to drive the enemy from the land and he comes to steal and plunder our harvest.

I believe there is a season for fighting and a season for harvesting. Right now is the season of battle. I believe that God is saying to the Church, "Don't try to gather the harvest until you've won the war! First you need to clear the land and take the territory, then plant your seeds and then you will reap the harvest." In time the season for harvest will come. In Isaiah 2:4 we see a reversal of the command given through Joel:

> He will judge between the nations
>   and will settle disputes for many peoples.
> They will beat their swords into plowshares
>   and their spears into pruning hooks.
> Nation will not take up sword against nation,
>   nor will they train for war anymore.

Here we see another day prophesied. A day of breakthrough, a day in which the presence of God is so apparent, a day of new wine—in other words, a day when the enemy's yoke has been broken and his influence shattered. In that day we will not need to use our weapons of warfare; we will be ready to take up our plowshares and begin harvesting!

Your personal battle

In terms of our lives as individual believers, I believe that many are being called to step into a new level of destiny in their lives. There is a sense that God is calling you to a new day and a new season in your life. But as you seek to break through and experience new depths in God, you will be met with new levels of opposition. If God has a plan for your life, then so does the devil! And if you are going to fulfill the potential of God for your life, then you are going to have to learn to fight to defend your harvest fields.

With each new level of revelation in God comes a new level of resistance. Have you ever noticed that when God has really spoken to you and you feel so excited about what He is going to do—often that is the time when you suddenly run into trouble? Suddenly the enemy whacks you out of the blue. What has happened? You have entered a new level of destiny and encountered a new level of warfare in the army of the Lord.

This is why we need to upgrade our skill in warfare as we progress with the Lord. The fact is, you cannot continue to fight like an army private if God is calling you to a higher rank! If God has given you the authority of a general in His army, then you need to learn the warfare of a general. First Timothy 6:12 says,

> Fight the good fight of the faith. Take hold of the eternal life to which you were called when you made your good confession in the presence of many witnesses.

What is this verse saying? We know that we have a calling and a destiny, but we have to fight for it! So many Christians do not want to engage in the fight for their destiny and their future. But if you do not engage, then the enemy wins by default. You may feel relieved that you are not caught up in warfare, but ultimately you are the loser. You only create a false peace of surrender by not fighting. You must fight the good fight and win. Then you will know peace—the peace of victory because you have won, not a false peace because you have abstained.

Many Christians have not fulfilled their destinies because they got into a battle with the enemy, things got a bit rough and they shrank back from the battle feeling intimidated. No! You must engage and fight for what is yours. Notice how often the apostle Paul provokes his spiritual son Timothy to stay in the battle and not give up. We have read of one instance above. Here is another exhortation:

> Timothy, my son, I give you this instruction in keeping with the prophecies once made about you, so that by following them you may fight the good fight.
>
> 1 Timothy 1:18

This time Paul is encouraging Timothy to remember the prophetic words that have been spoken over him and to be obedient to those words, to fight for their fulfillment. Paul was urging him: "There is a prophetic destiny on your life. Don't get lazy and sit around; push through! Keep fighting to possess it! Don't give up!"

It is God who equips us and makes His power perfect in our weakness; all we need to do is make the decision that we will fight!

Misconceptions about spiritual warfare

I want to move on to deal with a few misconceptions that many believers seem to have regarding spiritual warfare. These are concepts that I hear spoken around me frequently and we need to examine them and see if they are valid responses.

1. "I don't want to be involved with spiritual warfare"
People tend to think they have a choice about being involved with spiritual warfare. They tend to operate on an unwritten

principle that goes something like, "If I don't bother the devil, he won't bother me." That is a dangerous way to operate. The enemy does not follow rules! Just because you ignore him does not mean that he will ignore you. The fact is, we have a real enemy and we are at war, so we have no choice but to be involved. If the United States declared war on Britain, then whether you agreed with it or not, you would still be at war even if you wanted peace! In the same way the decision to declare war has already been made. On the cross Jesus declared war on the enemy and all his works, and He has not signed a peace treaty with the devil since. So if we are citizens of the Kingdom of God we are at war with the kingdom of darkness. Just by belonging to God's Kingdom means we are at war with the devil. The decision has been made for us!

2. "I'm not an aggressive person, so how can I fight?"

Some people by their nature are much more passive than others. Others like to be involved in mercy ministries, but not in the battle to free people's lives from their addictions. Warfare is for other people who they think are "that way inclined." But do we have a choice in the matter? Is it an either-or situation? Too often in the Church we have displayed the face of the Lamb to the devil and the face of the Lion to people! But God wants us to have the roar of the Lion of Judah in our mouths against the enemy in our land. We all can have a warrior spirit because we are all part of God's army, just as we are part of His family. This warrior spirit is not connected to your natural personality but a reflection of the character of God. Some women feel they do not relate to the "warrior" aspect of prayer. But I am sorry, ladies—I believe that every woman has a tiger in her tank. I know that even the quietest woman can be provoked to shout—just you bully her kids! We need to ask God to show us what the enemy is doing in our family or neighborhood. You cannot let the devil come onto your turf and bully your community! If you do not feel like you are much of a warrior, then ask God to let the warrior spirit rise up in you.

Proverbs 28:1 says,

> The wicked man flees though no one pursues,
>   but the righteous are as bold as a lion.

This boldness comes from recognizing your identity in Christ. It has nothing to do with your natural personality. It is simply who you are in Him! It is a characteristic conferred on you by God because He Himself is a warrior (see Judges 3:1–3). Here God shows us that He has left enemies in the land because He wants to teach those who have not yet had battle experience how to go to war. So get ready. God will train you to be a bold warrior!

3. "Spiritual warfare is just for prayer meetings"

Some people have a very strange view of spiritual warfare, thinking that it is something that we can switch on and off when we feel like it. We have the idea that spiritual warfare is *something you can choose to attend* and do at a Friday-night prayer meeting at church. But just as in the army you cannot choose which time of day your nation is at war to suit your convenience, neither can you clock in and out when you feel ready for some spiritual warfare. It is not about meetings. We need to realize that warfare is about everyday life.

A few years ago something really struck me. It was the fact that many Christians I knew always seemed to have disasters on their vacations! They would set off expectantly on their long-awaited holiday, but come back more exhausted than when they left. Things would go wrong: Plane connections were missed, the hotel was terrible, the food was awful, they ended up fighting with their spouse, they got sick, and so on.

Why is this? I thought. The answer came immediately. We have a mentality that separates work and ministry from our leisure time. When we go on vacation, we say to ourselves, *Okay, this is my time, I can do whatever I like, eat whenever I want and read different things.* While enjoying our relaxing holiday, we do not take the time to read our Bible all week because we see it as part of the "routine" that we are wanting a break from. Maybe we don't observe our usual prayer time; we just decide that it is our vacation and so we stay in bed.

I am not saying that we should never have any "downtime," but I am saying, "Don't forget you're in a war!" Do not be complacent, because while you have put your spirit into neutral, your enemy is out there prowling around, wanting to cause you harm. He does not call a truce because you have decided to take a vacation! We have to be on our guard all the time because our enemy is a terrorist.

4. "I have shouted and prayed loudly but nothing happens"

I have been to many prayer meetings where the effectiveness of the spiritual warfare was judged by the noise level being achieved—i.e., the noisier the better! Effective spiritual warfare is not so much about making a lot of noise, being aggressive or shouting, but more about your authority gained by your attitude. The greatest weapon you have in the place of warfare is your righteousness, your humility and your sacrifice.

We need to learn to come in the opposite spirit to the spirit of this age. Spiritual warfare is about turning a light on in the darkness. We read in Romans 12:20 an amazing statement by the apostle Paul:

On the contrary:
> "If your enemy is hungry, feed him;
>> if he is thirsty, give him something to drink.
> In doing this, you will heap burning coals on his head."

Notice how Paul begins: "On the contrary"; in other words, do the opposite of what would be expected. Whatever spirit comes against you, find the opposite in the grace of God. When you love someone who hates you—that is spiritual warfare. When you bless someone who is cursing you—that is spiritual warfare. Go in humility instead of pride; boldness instead of fear; servanthood instead of selfishness; generosity instead of a poverty mentality. A Christlike attitude has authority and power against the devil. It is not just about shouting! Our words must come out of a lifestyle of spiritual alignment with God. It is no good shouting at the devil about the sexual perversion in your community and then going home and watching an X-rated movie! Our lives need to demonstrate a godly lifestyle, which gives us holy ground from which we can confront the devil. However, I am not afraid of shouting and I do believe we need to declare His word with authority and there is a time to shout! Sometimes you can feel the indignation of God and your mouth becomes His mouthpiece to speak His word against the enemy.

5. "I feel like I'm fighting demons all the time. Is this healthy?"

Usually most of us are not fighting principalities, powers or territorial spirits in our everyday life, but we are fighting what is going on between our ears! The main battleground of spiritual warfare is our minds and our major enemies are doubt and unbelief! This is where Christians need to learn to fight efficiently.

Again, I think too many people quickly blame every situation they have on a demonic problem. They are focusing on the hoards of demons they imagine are surrounding them and lose the battle to keep their minds focused on Christ. Do not go demon hunting! Instead, make Jesus the focal point of your attention. I believe that we do experience both negative and positive spiritual atmospheres. There are definite places where you can sense the presence of evil and we need to pray to remove these demonic atmospheres. I do believe we should pray in order to pull down strongholds in the spiritual realm—I believe this is our responsibility as believers—but I also believe we must not become so distracted with the demonic world that we lose sight of Jesus in our everyday life. So although there is a real spiritual battle for the spiritual atmospheres in our land, we must first conquer the battle for the mind.

Paul makes this point in 2 Corinthians 10:3–5 when he says,

> For though we live in the world, we do not wage war as the world does. The weapons we fight with are not the weapons of the world. On the contrary, they have divine power to demolish strongholds. We demolish arguments and every pretension that sets itself up against the knowledge of God, and we take captive every thought to make it obedient to Christ.

And again in 2 Corinthians 4:4:

> The god of this age has blinded the minds of unbelievers, so that they cannot see the light of the gospel of the glory of Christ, who is the image of God.

Until we recognize the importance of the battle that takes place in the mind and learn to win it, we will never live victoriously. The devil wins most battles one thought and one temptation at a time. That is why Paul exhorts us to take *every thought* captive. If we do not, then each wrong thought becomes like a brick that the enemy uses to build a wall of separation between us and God.

Schemes of the enemy

If we are to be effective in winning our personal, daily, spiritual battle, it is important that we understand the schemes of the enemy and are prepared to counteract them. There are three areas in which the devil persistently manages to trip up unbelievers. It will help us to live with an awareness of these ploys so that we can be on our guard against them.

1. Fear and intimidation
The enemy will often try to intimidate us and make us afraid in order to prevent us from moving forward. But where does that fear live? In our minds. You need to deal with that fear whenever you are confronted with it. Pray, "Father, please deliver me from all my fears," and allow the Holy Spirit to touch and renew your mind.

2. Guilt and condemnation
The enemy always tries to mock us and remind us of our past failures. But we need to learn to walk as forgiven people, with our heads up and our shoulders back, knowing we are forgiven. There is a huge difference between conviction and con-demnation. *Conviction* is of the Holy Spirit and is specific; *condemnation* just makes you feel bad about everything and comes from the devil as an accusing spirit. So, do not be condemned but walk free.

3. Unforgiveness and offenses
This third tactic of the enemy is one that "locks up" so many Christians. Over the years I have seen many people who were

sick, subsequently restored, once they forgave a person toward whom they had held bitterness for a long time. Forgiveness was the key to their healing! Unforgiveness and offense is a major tool of the enemy to divide homes and marriages. We must learn to confess our sins to God quickly and to forgive people quickly when we are hurt and offended. There is great power in forgiveness.

Recognizing the battleground

> Therefore I stationed some of the people behind the lowest points of the wall at the exposed places, posting them by families, with their swords, spears and bows. After I looked things over, I stood up and said to the nobles, the officials and the rest of the people, "Don't be afraid of them. Remember the Lord, who is great and awesome, and fight for your brothers, your sons and your daughters, your wives and your homes."
>
> Nehemiah 4:13–14

In the last two chapters I will be looking at the area of strategic prayer for cities—spiritual warfare on a corporate scale. But before we attempt to enter that battleground, we need to be aware of our more immediate battleground: the home. I believe the importance of guarding the home is one of the main reasons God has been waking up the Church and urging people to start neighborhood prayer watches. Most of us are vigilant to protect our homes against theft, but how vigilant are we about guarding them from unwanted spiritual intruders?

We need to become territorial and mark our land; to learn how to pray and do battle for our homes, our sons and daughters, husbands and wives, brothers and sisters. God has put His authority on your life, clothed you with Christ, and you need to put on your spiritual armor and prepare to do battle!

Strategic Prayer for Cities—Part 1

There is a new sound of urgency resonating in the Church—it is time to take back our cities! It is time to see communities changed with the power of the Kingdom of God. For this reason, the last two chapters of this book will focus on practical prayer strategy for cities. We will systematically examine the book of Nehemiah because I believe this book holds such a strategy for rebuilding and influencing our cities.

The book of Nehemiah should be read in parallel with that of Ezra. This is important as here we see the prophetic gift of Ezra and the builder gift of Nehemiah working together for the sake of the city. Ezra was a prophet, more like a full-time church pastor with a national prophetic ministry in today's language, whereas Nehemiah was like a nine-to-five worker who had a full-time job as cupbearer to the king. But by working together they changed their city. This is what we see God doing again at this time. He is bringing together the Church leaders with the marketplace leaders so that by working together they achieve God's purposes for our cities. We will discuss this further as we proceed.

I believe God wants to establish a partnership between the marketplace and the Church so that we can fully impact our cities. We need to change our understanding of how cities are going to be touched by the presence of God and become places of His integrity. That is why I believe it is so important that an army of ordinary people begins to realize its critical role in this adventure of city-taking. Each one of us has a responsibility and a part to play—it will not just be one megachurch or an especially gifted preacher that will change the city.

Nehemiah hadn't been to Bible college, run a large church, or had a great ministry. He was a cupbearer to the king. He was in the catering business! And God suddenly turned his very ordinary world upside down.

Time for questions

One ordinary day, Nehemiah awoke and his life was changed when some fellow Israelites visited him from Judah:

> In the month of Kislev in the twentieth year, while I was in the citadel of Susa, Hanani, one of my brothers, came from Judah with some other men, and I questioned them about the Jewish remnant that survived the exile, and also about Jerusalem.
>
> Nehemiah 1:1–2

Suddenly on this day Nehemiah looked at his world and was disturbed by the Holy Spirit. He had been going to work for years, had his set routine, but this day it was different. He found he was thinking about his city of Jerusalem in a different way. He found himself beginning to ask questions about his people, his city. Similarly, I believe the Holy Spirit is disturbing us in the Church at this time. We are beginning to ask questions because the Holy Spirit is stirring something in us. He is asking questions of us such as, "Have you looked at your city? What is going on out there?" We can be so tunnel-visioned and only aware of our everyday life, that we become oblivious of the world around us. We go to church, listen to the sermon, go home, and our lives can be so disconnected from the lives of those around us in our community, at our workplace. Now the Holy Spirit is stirring the Church and challenging us to be connected with the real world. Consequently, believers are beginning to ask, "What is the true relevance of the Church to my life? Do the unsaved understand us? Am I making a difference? How is God going to turn our communities around? What are the needs of my community and neighbors?"

Sometimes as leaders we can feel threatened by such questions, but we need to understand they are not prompted by a rebellious spirit, but by the Holy Spirit. These uncomfortable questions are prompting us to challenge the status quo, causing us to wake up to a new agenda—a new focus and plan of God in these days.

Nehemiah was being provoked to ask these questions at two levels: First, he was concerned about his people, the Jews. We know that the Jewish nation is a picture of the Church—the people of God. So first, in these days, God is stirring questions in our hearts regarding the Church. The Holy Spirit is orchestrating a move away from individualism and toward cooperation. Churches are experiencing an increasing awareness of the people of God around them in the city—are the believers in other churches around us doing well, or badly? How can we work together to help one another? These issues are becoming relevant to us.

Second, Nehemiah asked questions about Jerusalem, the actual city itself. Have you been stirred to discover what is happening on your streets? Do you know what the crime rate is like? What are the pressures in the homes and on people's marriages? What pressures are facing the police? Do you want to get a better understanding of what is happening in your city? What does the name of your city mean? What does that strange-looking monument in the center of town actually signify?

If these questions have begun to stir in you, then you are connecting with the Holy Spirit's prompting as He provokes many of us to become aware of what is happening in our cities. I challenge you, do not just ignore these questions, because God has designed them to stir you from your comfort zone! They are a divine trigger that God will use to build a bridge between you and your community.

Nehemiah asks his visitors to give him a report on what was happening, and we read their troubling response in verse 3:

> "Those who survived the exile and are back in the province are in great trouble and disgrace. The wall of Jerusalem is broken down, and its gates have been burned with fire."
>
> Nehemiah 1:3

Nehemiah received the report and was dismayed. This same report could be given about Europe, America or Canada. In many nations the Church is in "great trouble and disgrace." God is moving in pockets in all these nations, but generally the status of the Church is weak and fragmented. There have been too many scandals involving sexual immorality; too many scandals regarding a lack of financial integrity; too much criticism and infighting with too little compassion expressed and real love demonstrated. The general report is poor. Ask the people on the street to write a report on the state of the Church and they will have some strong views on its ineffectiveness. We cannot simply blame the devil for deluding them! We have to take responsibility for the report and do something about it.

Recently I was talking to someone on a plane and he asked me what I did. I said, "I am a conference speaker and lecturer."

"What is your specialist subject?" he asked, so I said, "Super-natural communication." When I am talking to non-believers, I prefer to say this rather than "prayer" because it gives me an open door into their lives. I have found that people usually react negatively to the words *prayer* or *Bible teacher*, but they are fascinated with the concept of supernatural communication. Look in your local bookstore and you will see shelf after shelf filled with information on horoscopes, tarot cards and prophetic predictions. Everybody wants to be connected to knowledge greater than themselves; they want to tap into supernatural power.

I had a fascinating talk with this man about supernatural communication—about the possibility of connecting with the spiritual realm via the Holy Spirit. Finally, at the end of our conversation, this smart businessman asked me, "So you're into church?" "I am really passionate about Jesus and yes, I love church, too," I replied. "Oh, I gave church up a long time ago," he said. So I asked him why he had become so turned off by church. He told me, "When my Mom died I went to the church to try to find some comfort and to talk to my minister about it. But he refused to see me because he knew I was living with my partner at the time and we didn't want to get married. Afterward I thought, *If that's what church is all about, you can forget it.* I was going through a tough time and no one could care about me because I was not obeying their rules, which don't even make sense to me."

On that plane I realized that we have given out such wrong signals to people in the world. We often do not understand where they are coming from and cannot see beyond our church "rules and regulations." It may be uncomfortable for us to "read the report" of stories like this, but we need to know how people are viewing us. Many would write of the Church, "You're a disgrace. We've got no time for you."

Nehemiah is horrified by the report he receives. He knows that things are very wrong and he is grieved by it. He realizes that God's people and His house are a mess, but what about the city? The report came and it sounded something like this: "Nehemiah, the city is hurting, too. Community life is falling apart. The walls are broken down—those walls of the city, which represent protection, security, are gone.... The sense of safety and security is gone—if you go walking out at night, you are fearful you will be mugged. Crime is on the increase. There is no respect for older people."

The report Nehemiah heard was like the report you could read today about many of our modern cities. When we read in the news that a ninety-year-old woman was mugged by a gang of teenagers for just five dollars, then the walls of the city are broken down. Something has gone wrong with community life in the city.

The report also said that the gates of the city had been burned by fire. Gates represent *authority*. Our cities have lost their sense of honor and a respect for authority. Rarely do people wait for one another, stop to help each other or hold the door open for someone. We have lost our grace and manners. In schools across the United Kingdom you will find schoolteachers who are terrified of ten-year-old children who are out of control. And you do not have to visit tough, inner-city schools to encounter that culture of fear—it is widespread. Young teenagers are terrorizing classrooms because of a total lack of respect for authority. We need to rebuild the gates, but first we must acknowledge that they are broken down and face the consequences of this fact.

We have got to let the reports about our cities touch us. This is where it starts for the ordinary person—with those Holy Spirit questions.

Collect the statistics about your situation

Historians have discovered a new role in the Church as increasingly we are finding that *good intercession needs accurate information*. So this is the day for the detailed researcher to arise and equip the prayer ministry with accurate statistics and history. Today, intercessors have discovered the need to read and discover the background history and information concerning the places they live in. Maybe you hated history at school, but now you find a new interest and urgent sense to study your roots. It is a Holy Spirit thing. God wants to wake us up and show us how far our nations have fallen from their heritage and godly values. He wants us to listen to the report like Nehemiah did.

I believe that God is restoring the ministry of the "spy" to the Church! Remember when the people of Israel were on the journey to possess the Promised Land? The first thing Moses did was to send out spies (researchers) into the land who were instructed to find out all about it and bring back a report. Moses wanted a balanced report of both the good and the bad, so he would be well informed. Was this Promised Land as God had described? What were the battles that must be fought before they would have their land? Just like the Jewish people, God has given the Church many promises of a "promised land" and we need to go look at this land and see the promises.

Nehemiah's report was not a very positive one, but we need to keep a balance. In every city we will find the good, the bad and the ugly! The point is, we need a report that illustrates the full dimension. When the spies who were sent out by Moses brought their report, unfortunately ten of them could only see the bad and ugly side of things. Then they let their own report overwhelm them with fear. That still happens in the Church today. People say, "We're overrun by Masonic lodges and witches' covens; we'll never be able to change our city!" But wait a minute! We have the Lord Jesus Christ on our side. His blood is able to break the power of all sin. We must face the full facts about our city, but let's not become like one of the ten spies and spread doom and gloom throughout our churches. We also need to listen to the Caleb and Joshua heart that is full of faith—we must see beyond the report to a God who is strong, great and mighty, and well able to accomplish all He purposes to do. If we read all the crime statistics for London, New York and Los Angeles, we would never go outside, let alone believe for revival, but I believe that my Jesus died for those cities. His blood was shed for the people of the city of London, for New York, for Los Angeles. His blood is enough!

Look at Nehemiah's reaction to this report in verse 4. What does he say? When I heard these things I organized a committee meeting? I got the elders together? No, he says,

> When I heard these things, *I sat down and wept.* For some days I
> mourned and fasted and prayed before the God of heaven.
>
> Nehemiah 1:4, emphasis added

Nehemiah did not listen to the facts only with his mind—he listened with his heart and it touched his spirit deeply. In the West we are particularly good at assimilating information via our intellects, but poor at receiving it with our hearts and then responding. When we hear of a problem we immediately go into problem-solving mode because we are troubleshooters. But we cannot respond to what we hear about our cities just at an intellectual level; we need to let our spirits get involved. The fact is, what God most wants is to get at your heart, and for your heart to *feel* the report.

Just as Jesus could see both in the natural and the spiritual dimensions, so we need to ask God to open our eyes so that we can "see" our cities in the Spirit. In Matthew 9:35–37 Jesus walked through the towns and the villages and saw that the people were harassed and helpless like sheep without a shepherd. He was moved to compassion for them. Just like Jesus, you need to take the information you receive about your city and let it fuel your intercession.

Let information motivate you to intercession

Nehemiah wept when he heard the report and then for several days he mourned and fasted. The Bible does not tell us exactly how long he fasted, but we can see that Nehemiah immediately changed his priorities and gave himself to a time of fasting and prayer. God had taken hold of him and impacted his heart. The cry within him became a priority. Maybe Nehemiah lost track of time because this burden for his city consumed him. We do know that he was devastated.

Nehemiah knew there was a better destiny for his city. You know that there is a better destiny for your city. The majority of the people are not living what God purposed for them. There are wonderful verses in Zechariah 2:4–5 that I believe are God's heart for every city. These verses speak specifically about Jerusalem, but I believe this is God's intention for every city:

> "Run, tell that young man, 'Jerusalem will be a city without walls because of the great number of men and livestock in it. And I myself will be a wall of fire around it,' declares the LORD, 'and I will be its glory within.'"

I keep declaring this over cities because our cities have become so decimated. "Lord, put back Your wall of protection around them. God, be the gates of authority again. God, protect the city." *God loves cities because He loves people, and cities are where the people live.*

Nehemiah decides that the only solution to his problem is a

God-strategy. Similarly, I believe we need to take a lot more time in prayer to receive specific strategy from God on reaching our cities. I sincerely believe that God will give detailed strategy to those who are prepared to spend the time waiting and listening to Him. I remember when God first started speaking to me about the city of London. I had heard a bleak report. I had heard of so many good, anointed men, pastors working in London who were getting weary. They were having mental breakdowns, their wives were getting sick, they were having to withdraw; people were losing buildings, bankruptcies were happening, more and more good people were going under. It was like London was chewing up and spitting out ministry.

I began to respond to God and say, "Lord, this is not right. What can we do?" and God began to speak to me and say, "You need to provide a prayer shield for My people in the city, so that their backs are covered; so that they are not open to the onslaught of the enemy, because the enemy does not want to yield the capital city. The capital has authority and power. The enemy wants to retain the seat of government. You've got to learn to pray."

My initial response to God's strategy was, how *can I* do that? So, I began by approaching several of the large churches in London and sharing my vision with them and asking them to embrace it. In so many words they all said, "That's wonderful, but we can't get involved. We are working as hard as we can already." I went back to God disheartened and said, "Lord, the churches don't want to get involved with this." But He responded, "I didn't ask them to do it. I asked you to do it!" "How?" I asked, and God gave me a simple strategy to obey that would begin small and develop into something beyond my wildest dreams.

God told me to go to a prayer center in the countryside, take five people with me and spend three days there with no agenda, just listening to Him. He promised He would speak to us, and He did. By His Holy Spirit's power He allowed us to "feel" some of the pain He felt for the city of London. For the first day we mostly wept. That's all we did. We read through numerous emails each of us had received from various churches that were struggling—people who were in trouble— and they devastated us. We spread maps of London all over the floor and cried over them, soaking them in our tears. Eventually I cried out, "Lord, ten million people live in this city. How can we possibly do anything for them?" Then the answer came: "Divide the city up into twelve regions like you would slice a piece of cake." We began to do this and the M25 Londonprayernet (www.londonprayer.net) was born. God was revealing His strategy to us.

As we look back today to those early days in 1997, we realize that God has raised an army of ordinary people who take time to pray for London. At any time of day or night there are people who have taken one-hour slots and who pray for this city. If you look at the website www.londonprayer.net you will see what God is doing in London as people pray. It has been a privilege to work with members of Parliament, many church leaders and businessmen and see how God is touching the heart of this city, and we *will* see London turn.

I hasten to say, this method may not work for you. In fact, I'm almost certain it will not, because your city is different. God has a unique strategy to reach your city just as He does for mine. The most important thing is that we receive the report about our city and let that information motivate us to intercession. We need to listen to God and understand the steps that will guide us along the right path. Just as Moses went up the mountain and received an incredibly detailed strategy for building the Tabernacle, God is able to give us a detailed strategy for praying for our city. We need to get into that place of intimacy and listen to what He says, and it will involve some weeping and fasting.

People of many backgrounds are called to intercession!

I believe God is calling many different people into the place of intercession for our cities. Prayer for cities is not just for full-time pastors and ministers. Most of the people in our prayer armies are going to be everyday, nine-to-five people, because they are the people who walk the streets of the city. Those are the people who are out there in the marketplace, hearing what the people are saying. People with diverse grace gifts are needed to reach the diverse scope of a city, so today we need intercessors with different qualities, different emphases, to reach people effectively. In this section I want to look at some of those grace gifts. Each type of gift will respond, or be "triggered" to prayer, in a different way by the needs of the city.

The mercy gift
As these people walk the streets of their city they feel its pain; they see what is happening and they feel great compassion. They are drawn to be merciful for those in need in the city. Naturally speaking, this was not me, but I have learned compassion—the Holy Spirit has taught me mercy. I am a scientist by training—logical, systematic and administrative. I used to like paper more than people! But God got hold of me, turned my heart and made me compassionate. However, there are those who ooze mercy and compassion naturally because God has graced them with that. Their passion for people is the trigger that God uses to motivate them to the place of prayer for their city. We need these kinds of people to pray for our cities, because they find it easy to pray heartfelt prayers for others.

Leadership gift

These are the kind of people who, like Nehemiah, react to the report by saying, "Why doesn't somebody do something about it?" They see the mess and know that something needs to be done. They begin to think, to plan, to draw others in. It is their natural leadership gift functioning. They know that if they lead, people will follow. So there are those who come into the place of prayer because they know something needs to be done. In many senses prayer is not their first call; God got them "by accident" because of their desperation to see change. What triggers them to the place of prayer is their leadership skill, not their mercy.

Prophetic intercessory gift

For others it is the prophetic dimension that triggers them to pray for their city. Suddenly they begin to see things beyond the natural. Maybe they are walking down the streets and can see the streets full of young people; they see the potential of those young people, no longer a rabble going off to the bars to "hang with the boys," but a mighty, militant army of young people preaching the Gospel. They see beyond the natural to what could be; they see the harvest in the Spirit. These people look at the business community with all their resources and see what could be done with that money to further the Kingdom. The prophetic sees the potential. The cry of what could be beyond the natural triggers them to run to the place of prayer.

Research and practical action of prayer

Research about the history of a place can be the trigger that brings you to the place of prayer. As you begin to read the stories about your city's history, you may be moved to say, "Someone needs to do something! Someone needs to pray about this! Did you know that this happened in our town's past?" That research can be a trigger for prayer because God is using different things to get our attention.

Finance and faith gift

Many of the business community today are unexpectedly finding themselves in the prayer room. I am working to help a wonderful team of businessmen in Kristiansand, Norway. Some of them are in the fishing or shipping business and they have a lot of financial resources at their disposal. They began coming together to discuss one another's needs and pray for each other. One said to me recently, "I can't believe I get up at 6:00 A.M. on a Friday now for a two-hour prayer meeting. It doesn't make sense!" But God has got him in the prayer room. Why? Because he has realized that his resources and his influence can be used to extend God's Kingdom and he wants to get a strategy. Suddenly this man has a heart for his community and sees things that need to change.

Recently the mayor of Kristiansand approached these businessmen and the church and asked them to take over the running of a kindergarten school worth millions of Norwegian kroner. The school was failing, but now it is being run by this group of Christian businessmen with the church and is being turned around. These men are committed to prayer now because they have seen how God can release resources into the Kingdom when they pray.

In these days we need to be aware that different kinds of people are going to occupy our prayer rooms. It is not only going to be your "classic" intercessor. God is getting hold of all sorts of people from all sorts of backgrounds. Therefore, we are going to be having some different kinds of prayer meetings. We need researchers' prayer meetings, businessmen's prayer meetings, strategic prayer meetings. . . . The bottom line is that the Church needs to recognize that every person is called to the ministry of intercession, but within this gift there is a great diversity of expression.

Nehemiah's prayer of forgiveness and authority

In verses 5–11 of Nehemiah 1, Nehemiah prays an incredible prayer. Remember, this man is not a full-time minister; he usually works in the catering section! I believe as church leaders we need to recognize and release the authority that is on marketplace people to stand up in the place of prayer. When those Norwegian businessmen pray for their local authorities and their mayor, there is a tremendous authority as you hear them pray. When bank managers begin to pray about finance, when principals of schools pray for education, when chief surgeons stand up and pray for healthcare—all this is significant! Who better to pray than those who work in these spheres of the marketplace?

Nehemiah is the cupbearer to the king and occupies a place in the king's household. Now he stands up on behalf of his city and prays,

> "O Lord, God of heaven, the great and awesome God, who keeps his covenant of love with those who love him and obey his commands, let your ear be attentive and your eyes open to hear the prayer your servant is praying before you day and night for your servants, the people of Israel. I confess the sins we Israelites, including myself and my father's house, have committed against you. We have acted very wickedly toward you. We have not obeyed the commands, decrees and laws you gave your servant Moses."
>
> Nehemiah 1:5-7

In his prayer Nehemiah first acknowledges who God is and His awesomeness. He acknowledges by implication the covenant that exists between God and His people. He addresses what humankind has done to break that covenant. He confesses to God the sins that he says he and his forebears have committed—the generational sins that have broken the covenant.

He apologizes to God, saying, "We have acted wickedly; we have not kept our covenant; we have not done what is right." Likewise, if we examine the foundational covenants our Western nations have made with God, we also have to admit that we have not kept our side of the agreement. Our nations were founded on godly principles and the Bible was the reference book for most of our laws, but our recent forefathers have sinned. This is something that in the Western world we do not understand very well. We are very individualistic and do not have a strong sense of corporate identity and, therefore, corporate sin.

I grew up in an Eastern rather than a Western culture. I lived in India until I was sixteen years old. Eastern nations have a much greater understanding of their corporate identity and corporate responsibility. This is something we in the West need to learn, but we find the concept difficult to grasp. Among intercessors there is an ongoing debate about what is known as *identificational repentance*—i.e., repenting for the sins of our predecessors—and whether it is a good or a bad thing. (Appendix A covers this topic and explains my views on the concept.) Broadly speaking this is what Nehemiah does as he repents before the Lord. He confesses the sins that "we Israelites" have committed. He repents on behalf of his people. When was the last time we confessed to God the sins that *we* English, Americans or Canadians have committed when our nations have acted sinfully?

If you work systematically through Nehemiah's prayer, it provides a good model for praying for your city. Try following it as a pattern, taking it line by line and asking God, "What does this mean for me, my community, my city?" Your own situation will be slightly different from Nehemiah's situation, but pray it and see what God says to you.

As Nehemiah's prayer comes to a conclusion he says,

> "Give your servant success today by granting him favor in the presence of this man."
>
> Nehemiah 1:11

His statement means, "Now, I'm going back to work." Then, where you would expect the Bible to say, "Amen," it says, "I was cupbearer to the king." It is as if Nehemiah wants to let us know, "In case you think I'm something special, I'm just a cupbearer to the king."

Bringing alignment between natural and spiritual authority

At the beginning of chapter 2 we see that Nehemiah has returned to his day job, working for King Artaxerxes. I want to spend a little time looking at the typology in the relationship between Nehemiah and the king, because I have heard a number of different interpretations of it, and my view is probably different.

For instance, I don't believe, as some have suggested, that King Artaxerxes is a picture of the King of kings, our Father God. This king is a king of bondage, of captivity—a king that has taken hostage the children of God. He is a picture of an evil, natural king, not a spiritual, heavenly King. Therefore, in Nehemiah we see a picture of a man of God going up before *natural* authorities. The king represents authority on earth, *captive* authority, not God's authority. I believe exactly the same is true of Esther. I do not believe that when Esther approaches the king, in Esther 5, that he represents our Father in heaven. The scepter that she is seeking to touch is the natural scepter of authority that rules the cities, the land, the geography; it does not represent divine authority. Esther knew that she was approaching the seat of governmental power and authority in the land, the key figure of authority, so she needed to do so with extreme caution. That is why she asked her friends to pray and fast for her as she went.

In the same way, we need to have prayer, fasting, intercession and revelation before we approach those who are in governmental authority over us. We cannot just wander into the high places of authority in our cities and think the devil is going to say, "Nice to see you; here's the scepter of authority!" No, there is always a battle for the place of authority.

Just as Esther by her conduct won grace and favor with the king, so, too, Nehemiah had favor with the king because he was an exemplary employee. Plus, because of his position, he was easily able to approach and speak to the king. However, having prayed and fasted, the next time that Nehemiah was administering wine for the king, the king noticed that something was wrong with him and made the first approach:

> I took the wine and gave it to the king. I had not been sad in his presence before; so the king asked me, "Why does your face look so sad when you are not ill? This can be nothing but sadness of heart."
> I was very much afraid, but I said to the king, "May the king live forever! Why should my face not look sad when the city where my fathers are buried lies in ruins, and its gates have been destroyed by fire?"
>
> Nehemiah 2:1–3

I find these verses so significant. To me they speak of the effect that believers in the marketplace have on those around them. You might feel that you have been insignificant in your nine-to-five job, often wondering, *What in the world am I doing this for? All I do is go to work and I'm not achieving anything for the Kingdom.* But no—that's not right! You are building for yourself a credit account of favor when you do your job faithfully. If you go to work with a good attitude, even though at times you feel like you are working for evil King Artaxerxes, you are really working for a higher authority—the King of kings, Jesus! As you continue faithfully in your job, your boss will notice: "That guy has a good attitude. He's always happy, he has a good outlook, he never moans...."

If we go into the workplace carrying our authority in Christ, knowing we are working for the King of kings, then we will surely get people's attention before long. And we must do this, because if we do not have Kingdom people out there in the marketplace, how will we ever touch those thrones of authority in the city? Most of us long to see Christians in high places in government, in charge of schools, running hospitals. We need to encourage people in these callings.

In our nations we desperately need the *revivalist* anointing, like the Wesleys and Whitefields of days gone by who can preach the Good News of the Kingdom with power, but we also desperately need the *reformers*, too—those who are called to be rooted in places of governmental and societal influence; who have favor with those in high places of authority.

Nehemiah had that favor with the king and the king knew that something was wrong with him. At this point Nehemiah was very afraid. Was he going to make himself vulnerable to the king? Was he going to allow the king to see his true passion? He knew that if he said, "King, this is what I live for: I carry a city in my heart," there was a chance the king could react badly and Nehemiah could lose his job, or worse still, his head! But because of his relationship with the king over the years, guess what? He did not lose his head but rather he gained favor. He

told the king how disturbed he was about the well-being of his
city and the king's reaction was very positive.

> The king said to me, "What is it you want?"
> Then I prayed to the God of heaven, and I answered the king,
> "If it pleases the king and if your servant has found favor in his
> sight, let him send me to the city in Judah where my fathers are
> buried so that I can rebuild it."
> Then the king, with the queen sitting beside him, asked me,
> "How long will your journey take, and when will you get
> back?" It pleased the king to send me; so I set a time.
>
> Nehemiah 2:4–6

The king was also quick to ask, "When are you coming back?"
because he obviously valued Nehemiah as an employee. Because
Nehemiah had developed this relationship with the king, the
king was willing to give Nehemiah time off to go and do what he
needed to do.

A businessman I know who works for his local council is so
valued by his employer that his boss allowed him to work only
three days a week so he could spend the rest of his time planting
a church. His boss said, "I will do anything I can to make this
job easy for you, because I need you here!"

Nehemiah was not a classic revivalist preacher, but he was a
reformer. We need reformers out there in the marketplace if we
are ever going to see our cities changed. We need people who
can reach kings! People who can touch the heads of educational
services; people in government who will reform laws to reverse
ungodly standards in society. Like Ezra working with Nehemiah
and Wesley working with Wilberforce, we need reformers to
partner with the Church. Men like Wilberforce helped to stop
the slave trade; Lord Shaftsbury reformed society's attitude to
women and children; Elizabeth Fry reformed the prison system;
Florence Nightingale reformed the hospitals ... and so it went

on. All these reformers were working in the same season as the revivalists Whitefield and Wesley.

If there is a revival coming to our nations, then there must be reformers working in society, too. Come on, you Nehemiahs, do not get frustrated with the workplace—this is your moment! You might ask yourself, "Why has God kept me in this job?" But the time may be coming when the king looks at you and asks, "What do you need?"

Since he had the king's ear now and clearly his favor, Nehemiah pressed his advantage and told the king what he could do to help him if he was willing:

> "If it pleases the king, may I have letters to the governors of Trans-Euphrates, so that they will provide me safe-conduct until I arrive in Judah? And may I have a letter to Asaph, keeper of the king's forest, so he will give me timber to make beams for the gates of the citadel by the temple and for the city wall and for the residence I will occupy?"
>
> Nehemiah 2:7–8

Nehemiah gave the king a description of all the resources he would need and went on to say that "because the gracious hand of my God was upon me, the king granted my requests" (verse 8).

I believe the days are coming when we are going to knock on the doors of our local authorities and say, "We need this . . . ," and because we have won favor with them through our service, they are going to say, "We will give you what you need." It may be buildings, resources or people to help us, but we are going to see a reformation begin to happen.

Nehemiah 2:10 tells us that

> When Sanballat the Horonite and Tobiah the Ammonite official heard about this, they were very much disturbed that someone had come to promote the welfare of the Israelites.

The devil hates it when the Church gets out onto the street to promote the welfare of the people. God said this to me a little while ago: "The devil is never frightened of your good intentions, but he is terrified when you make the decision to go to work." I believe that is what God is stirring us to do in the Church in these days. We have had our prayer meetings, we have had wonderful prophetic visions, but what really terrifies the devil is when we begin to work out our prayers on the streets; when we begin to live out our prayers in the council offices, the schools and the workplace.

Many national governments have tried to outlaw prayer. They do not want prayer in schools or prayer gatherings on the streets. In the United Kingdom it is becoming more and more difficult to do outdoor evangelism. You now have to have a permit, and many local councils are refusing to give permits for outdoor gospel meetings. The enemy does not like it when we begin to work in the community. When our prayer gets worked out, we need to realize there is going to be some opposition.

Prayer on its own, however, is not enough. I have realized that "prayer" is the capital letter at the beginning of the sentence of history. Prayer is only the starting place. I do not want to pray for prayer's sake, I want to pray to bring in a harvest. I want to see God's Kingdom come on earth as it is in heaven. It is time for the reformers to get a vision of their destiny. Every day when you go to work you are helping to build the Kingdom. Every promotion you get is not just to give you a bit more money, but to give you a bit more favor, more influence in places of authority.

Once Nehemiah is back in Jerusalem, he begins to go out prayer walking at night and inspects the walls of the city. In verse 11 we read,

> I went to Jerusalem, and after staying there three days I set out during the night with a few men.

Nehemiah took a few people with him and began to see for himself what shape the city was in. As he walked around the streets of the city and looked at the walls that had been broken down, he began to see God's strategy for the rebuilding of the city.

Every time you begin to get complacent and you begin to think, *Our city's not so bad,* take a group of people and go out and walk the streets once again, especially at night. Allow the Holy Spirit to stir those questions in you again and remind yourself of the report. Let the atmosphere of your city and the information of the city life touch you again and trigger your desperation that will open the well of intercession once more.

Strategic Prayer
for Cities—Part 2

The day of rebuilding gates and walls

Throughout these final two chapters on strategic prayer for cities, I have deliberately kept the emphasis on general prayer strategy for the army of ordinary people, rather than discussing in depth the specialist topics such as spiritual mapping or identificational repentance. For more detailed information on these other aspects related to strategic prayer for cities, I suggest you read some of the books that are available by Cindy Jacobs, Ed Silvoso, Dutch Sheets and others. These are all part of the jigsaw puzzle God is bringing together as He reveals His corporate strategy to His people.

We ended the previous chapter looking at Nehemiah as a *reformer*. Revivalists are usually people who have a cry for the glory of God to be revealed in their communities. They have a passion for the spiritual state of the people. Reformers are looking at earth and what they see in their everyday lives and are bringing the Kingdom of God into their natural surrounding. *The revivalist looks in heaven and then earth; the reformer looks at earth and then calls to heaven!* So Nehemiah the reformer is looking at his city and then into heaven and bringing an alignment between the state of his city and the destiny call he knows God has revealed to him. Similarly, for each of us, God wants to take our natural giftings and skills and train us so that we can utilize them in a spiritual context.

For instance, I spoke to someone recently who told me that her company had sent her on a course to learn to speak Spanish. Although that skill was necessary for her job, at the time she thought it such a waste of time and a distraction from her passion to be more involved in her church. Some years later, however, a Spanish congregation started in this church and she was ready to help with the outreach ministry to the poor and needy. God has brought that person's natural training into alignment and now her language skills are being put to good use in the spiritual arena. You may not know exactly why God has been training you in a particular way, but there will come a day when suddenly the natural and spiritual come into alignment, and it all makes sense to you. Remember Joseph working in Potiphar's household, learning the administration skills of the Egyptian culture? He had no idea that he would be president one day and need these skills! So God taught him the basics of Egyptian culture, both in Potiphar's house and then in prison where he excelled. He found it was preparation to lead the nation in a time of crisis.

In Nehemiah 2, Nehemiah has been walking the streets of the city and praying, and gradually over those days of prayer-walking in Jerusalem a strategy was beginning to form. He was beginning to see his city and understand, "We need to rebuild," and God gave him a specific rebuilding strategy.

In Nehemiah 3 we find there are three main structures that Nehemiah was to rebuild—the walls, the gates and the towers of the city. I want to look at each of these elements and draw a parallel to what I believe God wants to do in our cities in these days.

1. The walls

What are the walls that God is calling the Church to build today? I believe the walls represent the army of ordinary people God is calling to prayer. The walls are the structure that connect the gates (representing authority) together and support them. They encircle the city and protect it. Each member of the Body of Christ across your city is one of these individual stones that is built into the wall that surrounds your city with prayer. We are called to be living stones built together in relationship for prayer, and as we get connected we fulfill a role for our city.

In every church you will find different people who have a heart for a specific sphere of society. There will be certain areas of authority that people naturally connect with. Maybe your interest is in the education gate; maybe the health gate. Even if you are not a leader in that arena, you know you have a heart connection with any issues in that area. So whenever that topic comes up as an issue for prayer, you find it easy to respond to. In this way you become part of the wall near the education or health gate, supporting the leaders who stand in this capacity on behalf of the city.

I believe God is raising up an army of ordinary people who are consistent pray-ers to build that wall of protection and security, because none of us alone can adequately cover all the prayer needs of our city, or even a specific sphere of city life—it takes an army of people all connected to one another to touch the gates of authority and make an impact.

This is what Nehemiah recognized as he began to rebuild the city. He began to station families at strategic points according to the area they related to. No single family rebuilt the whole city, but all families had to be involved and rebuild their part, nearest to where they lived. He sent Eliashib the priest to begin rebuilding the Sheep Gate. Then he positioned other families to rebuild the wall that connected to that gate. Why were the people stationed to rebuild the wall nearest to where they lived? What does that signify? One of the main reasons to have this wall was to stop the enemy coming in and ruining the city. So if they built the part of the wall nearest their home first, they knew their house would be safe from enemy attack! All of them had a vested interest in building this wall as it protected their home, by having a wall of protection covering their own back yard! You do not want the enemy coming near your house! We need to also understand this today—for example, if we have young children we should take an interest in rebuilding the walls of education near our house; maybe you are not called to change the whole education system, but you should be a voice of prayer in your local school.

So there is a sense in which, if you have a passion for a particular area (health, youth, etc.), then you will be motivated to help "rebuild" that part of the wall in prayer. You will want to make sure that part of the wall is secure and maintained. Nehemiah had recognized people's individual calling and ability, grouped them together and stationed them according to their natural interests and geography.

We need to do that in our cities. We are not all called to build the same things. This is true of individuals who attend their churches, but also of entire congregations. We need to recognize in the Body of Christ that certain churches have a specific bias for the sake of the city—some are more youth oriented; others are better equipped to reach the business community; others are effective in touching the poor and needy; others are moving in healing and wholeness. Each type of church needs to raise the prayer shield for the area it is called to. If members of the church are passionate about it, then they will do the job well.

Citywide prayer meetings, then, should focus on drawing

on those diverse giftings and allowing each church to pray for its section of "the wall." Many churches or individual ministries have tried to take cities by themselves and failed, but together, as we combine our strengths, we can take a city. I believe this is what God is looking for: an army of ready volunteers, like lots of little stones all connected and working together. We have to learn to fit together and support one another in our endeavors.

Some time ago while visiting Wales, God spoke to me as I was looking at the many stone walls that separate the fields. He said, "I'm not going to give you the luxury of cement! You are going to have to lean on each other." It struck me that as we build the walls together, there is not going to be a buffer zone. God wants to build us stone upon stone with nothing in between. This is a good illustration of the fact that there must be a level of transparency between us; we must be vulnerable and codependent. Another characteristic of stone walls is that the relative size of the stones is not important as long as they fit together. All stones of various shapes and sizes are positioned to bring security and to make up the whole.

Psalm 110:3 says,

> Your troops will be willing
>   on your day of battle.
> Arrayed in holy majesty,
>   from the womb of the dawn
>   you will receive the dew of your youth.

God is looking for an army of willing volunteers; He is not conscripting us. He does not say to us, "You have to do it whether you like it or not." He is looking for an obedient servant heart, for those people who will step up and say, "Yes, God, I will keep my place in the wall." As we build the wall together, consistency is so vital. Just like removing a stone from a stone wall will lead to instability, if you step back from your place in the wall, the gap is conspicuous. It brings instability and insecurity. Your presence is missed.

Ezekiel 22:30 says, "I looked for a man among them who would build up the wall and stand before me in the gap"—Why did God want that?—"on behalf of the land so I would not have to destroy it, but I found none."

Often this verse is used in the context of salvation, but actually its context is that of building a wall of protection, of standing in the gap on behalf of the land. Our God is a God who is interested in geography. He is into land, territory. He made the earth and all that is in it. He carved it, laid out the rivers and preplanned the exact format He wanted. The devil is also territorial. How did he grasp this principle? He learned this from the Creator of all things. And we, too, have to become territorial like our God and say, "This is my land, my geography given to me, and I want to put my feet on the land and stand in the gap on behalf of it."

By the time we reach Nehemiah 4, opposition is mounting against the Israelites from their enemies and Nehemiah has to take action. We read that half the people are working with their trowels while the other half are armed with weapons.

> I stationed some of the people behind the lowest points of the wall at the exposed places, posting them by families, with their swords, spears and bows.... From that day on, half of my men did the work, while the other half were equipped with spears, shields, bows and armor.
>
> Nehemiah 4:13, 16

To me this is a picture of the natural and spiritual coming together—natural tools working with spiritual weapons in prayer. God uses our natural abilities, but we have to learn the spiritual dimension, too. I believe God is waking that up in the Church today. As the army of ordinary people is busy working on the wall, God will begin to speak to it. As the people's hands are at work, heaven will open and they will be given the tools of the Spirit: revelation and prophetic insight.

As you work in your community, God will speak to you, and your prophetic insight will increase. Suddenly God will begin to show you the strategy of the enemy for your community and you will see what the enemy is doing around the walls, how he is trying to come against the gates. Revelation will begin to come and God will give you a strategy for rebuilding the walls. The army of ordinary people who began as workers will suddenly become an army of intercessors. Intercessors will begin to pray for their streets and for their people. They thought they were going to be doing some other work, but suddenly prayer will become their priority.

Isaiah 61:4 speaks of a people who will

> rebuild the ancient ruins
>   and restore the places long devastated;
> they will renew the ruined cities
>   that have been devastated for generations.

Who will do these things? Ordinary people who carry the Spirit of God. I believe that's what we are beginning to see in our cities today: people who are not your classic intercessors, who are busy working out in the marketplace when God speaks to them. The heart for our communities and prophetic revelation is growing in people more and more.

2. The gates

The two most notable things Nehemiah heard in the report were that the walls had been torn down and the gates destroyed by fire. All through Scripture "gates" signify places of authority and government. The city gates were the place where the elders of the city would sit and decide on business matters. From there the elders controlled what came into the city and what went out of it. The gates were a place where legal rulings were made, where righteousness was upheld, where disputes were settled. When Boaz wanted to marry Ruth, he went to the gates to settle the redeemer principle (see Ruth 4:1–11). Gates are mentioned 114 times in Scripture and always as a seat of authority, the place of decision making and government.

There has been a comprehensive attack on the gates of authority at every level of our society. The enemy has been burning the gates and they need to be rebuilt. Nehemiah 3 lists the different gates that provided entrance into Jerusalem, each of which had a different function. I believe these gates have parallels in our modern society and reveal to us the areas into which we should be praying as the Body of Christ.

For instance, the Sheep Gate, which historically was the area where shepherds congregated with their sheep and was rebuilt by the priests, speaks to me of the "church" gate of the city. We need shepherds/pastors in our city to care for the people of God, and we need believers with a concern to maintain the "sheep gate" who are committed to pray for these leaders— those who will pray for the restoration of godly shepherd-leaders in our communities and are prepared to function as stones in the walls that support that gate.

For the Fish Gate I see the parallel of evangelism. We need those who constantly reach out in prayer for the lost. The Old Gate represents generational authority and wisdom. There are Christians who are like statesmen—they carry respect and diplomatic skills of wisdom for the city. We need city elders, men of wisdom who will sit at the gates. The Fountain Gate speaks to me of healing, a place where miracles and medicine can come together.

But as we examine our cities, what is sitting at the gates? Is it godly government and wisdom? No, they have been burned with fire and evil spirits have occupied many of our gates— spirits of anarchy and rebellion. We need to go back and repossess those gates and see seats of righteousness restored. We need anointed men and women of God to sit at those gates and rule. If not, then who else might sit at the gates? The Masonic influence occupies so many of our city gates. We need to see these spirits move out of the gates and see the Kingdom of God move in.

What are the "gates" that hold the keys of influence and authority in our modern cities today? I believe they are:

- Commerce and financial institutions
- Law and order—the police, prisons and the justice system
- Social services and family
- Local government and political arena
- Health
- Universities—power to train the next generation of leaders
- Education
- Youth
- Church
- Tourism/nations—this allows people of diverse backgrounds with their different religious beliefs to influence our cities
- Media/journalism—this is a gate that has become so influenced by ungodly voices! It is one of the toughest gates to keep pure.
- Music/arts/theater industry
- Plus many others!

There are believers working in these spheres who really need our support in prayer. They often have authority and influence in these different spheres of society, so we need to function like a wall, and hold them up and protect them.

In Norway during the early 2000s, both the health minister, Dagfinn Hoybraten, and the prime minister were Christians. The health minister contacted us during this time and said, "We want to see prayer spread throughout our government. Will you help us?" That is exciting. It is a real example of godly authority functioning at the gates.

Can you identify the gates in your own community? What are the places of influence? Some cities or parts of the country are known for particular industries, for instance, printing (i.e., communication), commerce, leisure, and so on. Perhaps your city houses the headquarters of a cult or a false religion. It is a good idea to read up on your community and talk to the people who have lived there for years. Some of the most knowledgeable people in your community, town or city are the people on the streets. Ask them what or who are the major influencers in the city. Find out what are the gates of influence and then look for those who have a heart to pray about that sphere so that together you can begin to pray and rebuild the walls.

Once you discover what the gates are, ask God to show you what is sitting in those gates. Our education system is dominated by humanism, for instance. It is controlling our whole culture and even infecting the Church so that much of our thinking, without realizing it, has become subtly humanistic. The Church is becoming too politically correct. We are not just becoming seeker-friendly; we are becoming devil friendly!

What is sitting at the gates of finance in your city? For many, huge personal debt is a growing problem. At the time of my writing, the U.K. national credit-card debt is £56 billion. That does not include house loans or anything else, just plastic cards! [1] We need to bring back godly, biblical money-management principles into the gate of finance. How many homes and marriages have been decimated because of debt? We need revelation on what is controlling these gates so that we can move in an opposite spirit against them and demonstrate the principles of God.

Church and marketplace working together

I believe if we are ever going to take possession of the gates of the city there has to come a genuine and honoring partnership between the Church and the marketplace. For too long we have not respected Christian business people.

A few years ago I was leading a citywide celebration and from the platform I called for all the leaders in the city to get out of their seats and come to the front. I made it clear that the altar call was for *anyone* who had responsibility for a number of other people because of his or her job—business people as well as church leaders. I was deliberately being naughty because I had a plan in mind! When everyone was gathered at the front, pastors and nine-to-five workers side by side, I said, "I want to pray for every man or woman in a position of leadership who is responsible for more than five hundred people. If you don't fit into that category, would you please sit down."

Most of the church leaders had to go and sit down and the people who remained at the front were mostly business people, the majority of whom were ten or fifteen years younger than the pastors who had come forward. I went along the row asking people their ages and the youngest person in that group was a woman of 29. She was unmarried and already a regional director for her company. She was not sure exactly how many people came under her authority, but it was over one thousand.

I admit I was being a little bit provocative, but what I was trying to illustrate to those assembled was that we have limited the word *leader* to just those serving in a spiritual capacity. But what about all those Christians who are leaders in the natural sector and have huge opportunities of influence? If a *leader* means a person who is leading other people, then we have many, many Christian leaders out there, thousands of them! But somehow the Church has dislocated itself from those within its ranks who have significant leadership skills and are leaders in the marketplace—and these Christians have felt so unsupported.

For example, I have a friend who works in the city of London who is connecting all the time at a very high level in the finance/banking world. Because of her job she often cannot make it to church on a Sunday morning. In her local church she was considered a poorly committed Christian because of her Sunday attendance. Yet, not many of her congregation knew that there was a period in her life when God got her up an hour early every day to go into her office and pray over every desk of her junior staff. For five years she did this, getting up at 4:00 A.M. every morning to be in the office by 5:00 A.M., so she could pray for everyone who worked in her offices. Yet, according to a church leader, because she was not in church on a Sunday morning she was not a good church member. From his perspective she was not "leading" anything in the church, but all her work colleagues rated her as one of the best leaders they ever had.

My friend got promoted and that meant she was working in New York one week, Tokyo the next, Frankfurt the next and then London. With that kind of job you just cannot be in church every Sunday morning. We need to have a different attitude toward supporting this kind of industry leader. If we want Christians in places of influence in society, then something has got to happen so that the walls and the gates work together. If you have a Christian prime minister, he is not going to be in your church every Sunday morning! Our attitudes have got to change.

Make a start by asking God to give you connections with people who sit at the gates—to connect you with Christians in the marketplace who have leadership positions. God may also show you the Cyrus leaders, the people in leadership who are not Christians (yet!) but who do have a heart to bless and do good to the Church. Befriend them, begin to build up your wall next to their gate to support them and let's begin to hold up these gates. Too often we have been in conflict with one another instead of cooperation. In fact, at times it has even been a gender issue: Many of those involved in intercession have been women and many of those in both the Church and marketplace leadership roles have been men. To put it simply, often the male leadership quality has rejected the female revelation/prophetic quality. A lot of women who have had genuine prophetic revelation have been called "Jezebel," as though they were trying to manipulate the leaders and tell them what to do. If leaders suspect that to be the case, then immediately their defenses go up. Equally, the prophetic intercessors have been hearing from God and have been unwilling to share strategy with marketplace leaders because they assume that they will not listen. Then women have resorted to methods of supernatural superiority and manipulation, which have damaged the leaders. So, both genders have reacted poorly.

Those in positions of leadership can at times feel threatened by intercessors. They can be wary of the prophetic revelation of others because they tend to think, *We are supposed to be in charge here!* and do not like being told what to do. When this resistance exists, leaders tend to try and operate out of their own governmental authority instead of listening to divine revelation. They devise programs or call committee meetings to decide the way forward, because "government" can always create a plan and implement it.

Consequently, the enemy has a field day. Intercessors and

leaders have been effectively separated from one another. We have had a situation in the city where all those with spiritual leadership roles meet together at leaders' meetings, and all those whose job it is to support the gates have congregated together in separate prayer meetings. These two groups of people have not met and worked together. Consequently, very little has been built! If you have gates without walls, then you have no support, nothing to hold them up. If you have only walls but no gates, then you are going to go mad! You have placed crazy people in a room with no doors!

In these days, I believe that God wants to break that suspicion down and bring us back together, shoulder to shoulder, so that we support one another. The gates must begin to trust the prophetic revelation of the walls, and the walls must respect the authority of the gates.

Relationships between the gates (leaders) and the walls (intercessors)

Until we begin to see government and revelation working together, I do not believe we are going to effectively reach our cities for the Kingdom. That is why God is increasingly encouraging pastors and intercessors to meet together. This is a new day of cooperation between leadership and prayer warriors. Throughout Scripture a number of leader-intercessor relationships are mentioned and it will be helpful to look at a few examples.

▶ *Moses, Aaron and Hur*

Exodus 17 provides us with a lovely picture of what this working together looks like. The Amalekites are attacking the Israelites at Rephidim. Joshua is leading the Israelite army and Moses, Aaron and Hur ascend the mountain to survey the battle and to intercede for their people.

The mountain signifies intimacy time with God. How often do leaders allow key intercessors to go away on a leadership retreat with the rest of the leadership team? In this Scripture we see the leaders and the intercessors working together. Aaron the high priest, a prophetic intercessor, accompanies Moses, the leader, up the mountain.

God's people are in difficulty because the enemy, the Amalekites, have come into the valley. The valley is always a picture of everyday life in the Bible. It is the place of challenge while the mountain is a picture of connectedness to God. Joshua is busy doing his job in the valley, fighting the enemy. Moses the leader knows that the enemy is seeking to destroy them and recognizes his people are being overwhelmed. He knows that he needs a strategy for breakthrough. Moses also knows that his governmental authority is not going to be enough to win the day, so he takes Aaron and Hur with him and together they go up the mountain.

> So Joshua fought the Amalekites as Moses had ordered, and Moses, Aaron and Hur went to the top of the hill. As long as Moses held up his hands, the Israelites were winning, but whenever he lowered his hands, the Amalekites were winning. When Moses' hands grew tired, they took a stone and put it under him and he sat on it. Aaron and Hur held his hands up— one on one side, one on the other—so that his hands remained steady till sunset. So Joshua overcame the Amalekite army with the sword.
>
> Exodus 17:10–13

Previously in verse 9 Moses had said, "Tomorrow I will stand on top of the hill with the staff of God in my hands." Moses was holding God's mandate in his hands. The staff was the symbol of God's authority on Moses. It was given to him as a sign that

God had called him. Aaron and Hur stood alongside Moses and held up his hands. Notice they did not take the staff from his hands; rather, they supported him while he held it. Good intercessors do not try to take the authority away from their leaders, but they hold their hands up and support them. Too often intercessors try to take the staff because they feel they know what to do. No, our job is to hold the leaders' hands. Notice that Aaron and Hur got Moses to sit down. They allowed him to rest in his authority.

As long as they held that position, the battle was won. I believe this is symbolic of the position of the walls working with the gates and serving our cities. Many of our businesses are fighting through and battling in the marketplace and they frequently become exhausted. They do not need us to offer them solutions; they just need our support. They need us to hold their hands up. They do not need the Church to grab the staff out of their hands. We need to learn to take the role of Aaron and Hur.

▶ *Esther and Mordecai*

We see a similar thing in the book of Esther when Esther and Mordecai work together. Esther had insight and revelation herself, but she obeyed Mordecai's instructions. At other times she shared her revelation with Mordecai. She was constantly looking to him to receive her instructions, and he continued to impart wisdom and instruction to work alongside her revelation until she finally stepped into her purpose and destiny.

I want to say to all intercessors: Let leaders direct you and give you wisdom and strategy. They may say to you, "Don't push that too hard, be careful, wait," and so on. Don't react negatively—they are not trying to control you, they are trying to protect you. When Mordecai and Esther were working together in a partnership, sometimes Mordecai obeyed Esther. At other times it was Esther being instructed and Esther did what she was told. There was a mutual trust and respect, so instruction could flow both ways. Ultimately, both of them were able to step into their full destiny. Often we only talk about Esther, but Mordecai stepped up, too, and received the signet ring of leadership. He became a leader in the land.

As leaders, we really need to let God form those prophetic partnerships. It does not mean we are less of a leader if we take instruction from intercessors. And intercessors, it does not mean we are controlled if we receive wisdom from our leaders.

▶ *Paul and Lydia*

In Acts 16:14–15 we read of a woman named Lydia who helped the apostle Paul:

> One of those listening was a woman named Lydia, a dealer in purple cloth from the city of Thyatira, who was a worshiper of God. The Lord opened her heart to respond to Paul's message. When she and the members of her household were baptized, she invited us to her home. "If you consider me a believer in the Lord," she said, "come and stay at my house." And she persuaded us.

Here we see a slightly different kind of relationship. Paul, the apostolic leader, has come to the city to teach the believers there. The intercessor, Lydia, says, "Come and stay in my house. Let me make you welcome here."

As we see apostolic gifts coming to the city, the cry of the intercessor needs to be one of welcome: "Come and stay with us." Intercessors need to be people who can be trusted, not people that our leaders are always worried about.

3. The Towers

I believe, like Nehemiah, that the rebuilding of the walls and gates is of prime importance, but there is a third structure mentioned in Nehemiah 3, which is the towers. The towers were the places where the watchmen of the city were stationed to keep watch, especially for approaching danger. From that vantage point they could walk around the top of the wide walls and have a panoramic view of the landscape both outside and inside the city. Isaiah 62:6 says,

> I have posted watchmen on your walls, O Jerusalem;
>   they will never be silent day or night.

For us today the towers represent those in the Body of Christ who have a watchman anointing—that strategic, prophetic anointing that alerts the Body of Christ to areas of danger or need. As we rebuild the walls, then God can anoint those watchmen to stand on top of them. They stand secure on that layer of prayer and keep watch for the people. Cindy Jacobs is a good example of a person with this anointing. Although she was part of the wall, she now stands upon the wall and has become a watchman for nations.

This is why it is so imperative that we raise that army of ordinary people around our cities. Without this army we are never going to establish watchmen on the towers. We need that secure place for people to stand and see what the enemy is doing. When you stand on a wall, your perspective totally changes. You can see much more. The enemy cannot approach too close when someone is watching from a high vantage point, as opposed to being on the ground. Churches need to develop this prophetic ministry that can bring guidance and alert them of any danger.

The city belongs to God!

Why in these days do we hear so much talk of prayer shields and prayer nets? Because in these days God is giving us a strategy that will allow the prophetic gifts a place to function and also protect our leaders. Our cities belong to God. God is placing a new attitude in His Church concerning the geography, the land. God wants to put a sense of commitment in our hearts, a new responsibility for our communities. We know well the exhortation of 2 Chronicles 7:14:

> "If my people, who are called by my name, will humble themselves and pray and seek my face and turn from their wicked ways, then will I hear from heaven and will forgive their sin and will heal their land."

God is still calling us to humble ourselves, to seek His face and pray. That word *seek* has a strong meaning. It means to give ultimate priority to; to have a single eye; to be devoted and focused on; to watch for the slightest of movement. That is seeking. It means not letting God out of our sight.

But we must also turn from our wicked ways. Unfortunately, what is in the world has entered the Church. God woke me up one morning with this warning for the Church: "Gossip and competition are luxuries that the Church can no longer afford." Yet, if we turn away from wickedness, God promises that He will hear from heaven. He will forgive our sins and He promises to heal the land. Our corporate sin ruins the land and our very geography is groaning and crying out because of the burden of sin that has contaminated it.

Sometimes people may think I am being too extreme by saying that, but read Leviticus 18:1–23 and compare it to our modern society. This is a chapter in the Bible that you would rather your children did not have to read. It goes into explicit detail about every kind of sexual sin that man practices that is an abomination to God, including incest and sex with animals. The Bible is blunt and it is very up-to-date. It is relevant in the 21st century. Then, in verses 24–27, it says,

> "Do not defile yourselves in any of these ways, because this is how the nations that I am going to drive out before you became defiled. Even the land was defiled; so I punished it for its sin, and the land vomited out its inhabitants. But you must keep my decrees and my laws. The native-born and the aliens living among you must not do any of these detestable things, for all these things were done by the people who lived in the land before you, and the land became defiled."

The Bible says that the defiled land vomits out its inhabitants. Have you ever felt that the place where you are living is spiritually hard? Every time you try to do something it is like the very land resists you? The land is sick and needs healing. That is why God is moving Christians back in to occupy the cities. We need to get a vision for our cities. God got hold of me and gripped me with a vision for the city of London. He wants to do the same with you. He wants to walk you through your city and show you how devastated and ruined it is, what the enemy has done to it. You are part of His army of ordinary people and you are His answer for the rebuilding of communities. You are going to be one of the glory carriers. God is going to use you—one of an army of ordinary people—to change the face of cities and nations.

So, come on—why don't you take a few more minutes and let us pray together? God wants to stir a new passion for prayer in your life. He wants to anoint you with the joy of prayer and a language of supernatural communication that will touch heaven and change your world. God has called you and will equip you to be a part of His army.

> Right now in the precious name of Jesus, I pray that the Spirit of God will touch you and strengthen you in your prayer life. Today, Father, I ask You to equip us on our prayer journey and let our prayer become a place of delight and joy.

I trust that as He touches your life, you will have the courage to make the tough choices you need to make and implement these adjustments so that you can do all He has called you to do. Let God awaken in you a fresh heartcry and let Him touch you with His heart of compassion for people. Let the Lion of Judah arise and break the power of the enemy.

> So come, precious Jesus, and open our eyes so that we can see our neighborhoods and hear their cry and see the harvest. Let us be those who influence our cities with the presence of God. Lord, here I am; use me, I pray! Amen.

God bless you, and thank you for sharing my prayer journey with me in this book. Thank you for being a partner with me in this incredible army of ordinary people. I do believe that together we will see His Kingdom come and His will done in our cities, and this will give us great joy! Now it's up to you!

Note

1. Source: www.creditaction.org.uk/debtstats.htm.

Identificational Repentance

The term—identificational what?

The term *identificational repentance* (IR) was first used by John Dawson in his book *Healing America's Wounds* (Regal, 1994) and is defined as:

> A type of prayer, which identifies with and confesses before God the sins of one's nation, people, church or family.

The history of IR

IR can be clearly seen in the Old Testament Scriptures and was practiced by leaders such as Moses and Nehemiah as discussed in the final chapters of this book. The concept was recently revived by prayer leaders such as Cindy Jacobs and throughout Latin American churches. But IR is not new in the Church. Corporate confession of sin has been a well-established concept, distinct from individual confession, for nearly five hundred years of church worship in the Anglican Church. In the *Book of Common Prayer 1559* (the Elizabethan Prayer Book) there is the following prayer:

> Remember not Lord our iniquities, nor the iniquities of our forefathers. Spare us good Lord, spare thy people.... Lord have mercy on us.

The 1789 ratified *Book of Common Prayer* of the Episcopal Church in the United States also has the theme of corporate confession. It includes the Psalter—the Psalms designated to be used for morning and evening congregational prayers—which includes Psalm 106:6:

> We have sinned, even as our fathers did;
> we have done wrong and acted wickedly.

In his book *Anglican Public Worship*, published in 1953 by SCM Press, Colin Dunlop, former Dean of Lincoln, also articulated the nature of corporate identity and confession with these words:

> We make our confession as members of the Church ... we confess not only our private sins, but ... our share in that whole aggregate sin which all but crushed our Master in the Garden of Gethsemane.

Evangelical Christian leaders around the world continue to see the need for, and importance of, this practice.

Questions and answers

▶ *Isn't it a heavy and unnecessary responsibility for us to have to confess and deal not only with our own sin but then the sin of our family, church, nation, and so on?*

Scripture indicates that when confessing sin we should not be wading through a list of sins, whether personal, corporate or generational, but rather should respond in obedience to the Holy Spirit's instruction. Psalm 139:23, which says, "Search me, O God..." is one of many Scriptures indicating that the Holy Spirit should search us and reveal our sin to us. Similarly, 1 John 1:7–9 suggests that walking in the light with God will result in an ongoing process of confession and revelation concerning sin. This will be true for both individual and corporate entities. Confession of past sins, which the Holy Spirit shows us, is not an additional burden, but is often the very means God gives us to unburden ourselves from guilt and stubbornly entrenched patterns of sin.

▶ *Isn't IR the same as praying for the dead, in an attempt to absolve them of responsibility for their own sins?*

No, IR has nothing to do with absolving a past generation, but rather is a means of receiving God's grace to be freed from the consequences of the sins of the past that are crippling our present. Jeremiah's confession of past sins (see Jeremiah 3:25; 14:7, 20) led to him being spared with his servant Baruch from the captivity resulting from past sins (see Jeremiah 40:1–6; 45:2–5). In Deuteronomy 21:7–9, the Israelite elders could be freed from the guilt of bloodshed in their territory by renouncing any complicity with past murders and asking God's forgiveness by means of a sacrifice.

Second Samuel 21 is the classic IR scripture, where God showed David that the famine in the land had nothing to do with David's generation but was rather the result of Saul's action in a previous generation when he broke the blood covenant with the Gibeonites. A curse had, therefore, come on the land and only David's IR was able to break the curse and enable God to return His blessing to Israel.

IR is also a means of accessing God's grace on a corporate

level to others, thereby enabling nonbelievers to repent more freely of their own sin and come to Christ. Jesus prayed for His persecutors on the cross, and Moses, Ezra and Nehemiah all prayed in the same way over past sins of the people.

▶ *Is IR really biblical? Does the New Testament (NT) tell us to follow the Old Testament (OT) model of confessing corporate, generational, national and personal sin?*

First, the only Bible in the early Church was the OT, so all their concepts of confession and repentance were taken from the OT. As Paul wrote, "All Scripture [referring only to the OT] is God-breathed and is useful for teaching, rebuking, correcting and training in righteousness" (2 Timothy 3:16). James 5:16 and 1 John 1:9 were written using the OT model of confession and repentance.

God's holiness causes Him to "[visit] the iniquity of the fathers upon the children" (Exodus 20:5; 34:7, NKJV), but His mercy longs to show compassion to this generation and to a thousand others! God's challenge in Ezekiel 18:20 and Jeremiah 31:29–30 is to break with the entrenched sin patterns of the past generations so He can bless them. Spiritual oppression results from generational sin (see Hosea 4:12–13), and is implied in Exodus 20:5 and 34:7 and Deuteronomy 5:9. The future generation is held captive by a demonic spiritual oppression and Satan has grounds to hold them because of past sin. When confessed and repented of, the oppression is lifted.

The biblical view of Leviticus 26:38–42 is that we should not only confess personal sin but also parental and national sin. Nehemiah 1:6–9 shows the biblical understanding that both are inseparable aspects of turning back to God. We see it also in Jeremiah 3:25; Psalm 106:6; Daniel 9:8, 20; Ezra 9:6–15; and Nehemiah 9:2.

Jesus, Paul and Peter all assumed that the OT model was still a reality, in passages such as Matthew 23:32–35 ("fill up . . . the measure of the sin of your forefathers!" [verse 32]); 1 Thessalonians 2:16 ("so as always to fill up the measure of their sins" [NKJV]); and 1 Peter 1:18–19, which states that the blood of Jesus saves us from the empty pattern of ancestral sin from our forefathers.

▶ *Don't Ezekiel 18:20 and Jeremiah 31:29–30 teach that we no longer share in the iniquity of our parents, and generational sin is not passed down?*

No, because a fundamental covenantal principle from Exodus 34:5–7 relates recycling of generational sin to be part of God's very character of holiness. The context is simply saying that children will be affected by, but not punished for, the sins of their fathers.

▶ *Why should we take responsibility for past sins in our family line, or nation, which we have not committed?*

We are a priesthood of believers and as such we need to identify with the roots of any given sin, and learn to bring sin to God so others can be free of the effects. Daniel, Ezra and Jeremiah prayed this way. We may not have had an abortion, but we can identify with the spirits that lead to abortion. Daniel 9 and 10 show us the way IR breaks the demonic oppression of principalities and powers, and it smashes the stronghold of the enemy.

▶ *Doesn't the Bible teach that we can only seek and receive forgiveness for our own personal guilt and sin?*

No, because we see that Moses appealed for forgiveness for all the people of Israel (see Exodus 32:9–14; 34:8–9; Numbers 14:13–20). Samuel said it was a sin for him not to pray for Israel regularly (see 1 Samuel 12:23), implying the kind of intercession you see in Ezekiel 22:29–30, where God looks for a man to stand in the gap for another's sin. In Exodus 8–10 Moses is able to intercede for the sins of Egypt. The cases of Moses, Ezra, Nehemiah, and Jesus on the cross show us the power released when we seek the forgiveness of others' sins—a way is open for them to find the Lord through repentance and faith.

▶ *Isn't the OT idea of generational sin, and confession of generational and national sin, foreign to the NT? Surely when the blood of Jesus covers our sins, we don't have to confess former sins?*

Matthew 23:32–35, 1 Thessalonians 2:16 and 1 Peter 1:18–19 all show the NT assumes an ongoing understanding of the OT concept of generational sin. Corporate confession is still a legitimate category of NT confession and practice. No NT passage contradicts the OT passages of confessing individual and corporate sin.

The plural nouns in 1 John 1:9 and James 5:16, "confess our [or "your"] sins," and NT passages that teach explicitly about the confession of sin, clearly include a sense of both individual and corporate confession. NT passages include nonspecific and nonexclusive language that would certainly include the notion of confessing corporate, generational and national sins, as well as confessing individual and personal sins. At least the corporate is certainly not excluded.

▶ *Is our real problem with the term* IR *to do with our poor understanding of being a corporate body/community and our ability for identification rather than repentance?*

All through Scripture there is such a sense of community. We are a body! If one suffers, we all suffer. The sense of IR is really our level of relationship with the community/city/land/ region. This is a grace thing, according to calling. It is difficult to confess if you do not identify. Maybe the reason developing nations have found IR easier is they have greater understanding of community/fellowship that we in the West have lost.

But all confession of sin must be Spirit-convicted and Spirit-led. It must not become a form of repetitive prayer, but an issue of genuine sorrow of the heart.

Books and references

Neil T. Anderson, *The Bondage Breaker*, Harvest House, 2000.

John Dawson, *Healing America's Wounds*, Regal Books, 1994.

John Dawson, *Taking Our Cities for God*, Creation House, 1990.

Francis Frangipane, *The Divine Antidote*, Arrow Publications, 1990.

Cindy Jacobs, *Possessing the Gates of the Enemy*, Chosen Books, 1994.

Cindy Jacobs, *The Voice of God*, Regal Books, 2004.

Charles H. Kraft, *Defeating Dark Angels*, Vine Books, 1992.

Roger Mitchell and Brian Mills, *Sins of the Fathers*, Sovereign World, 1999.

Ed F. Murphy, *Handbook for Spiritual Warfare*, Nelson Reference, revised and updated edition, 2003.

Ed Silvoso, Global Harvest Ministries Magazine, testimonies of change.

C. Peter Wagner and Cindy Jacobs, articles written in *Wagner Prayer Track News*.

C. Peter Wagner, *Breaking Strongholds in Your City*, Regal Books, 1993 [see section by Bob Beckett].

C. Peter Wagner, *My Father's House and I Have Sinned*,
    Wagner Publications, 1995.
Tom White, *Believer's Guide to Spiritual Warfare*, Vine Books,
    1990.

Global Prayer Movements

All over the world there are encouraging signs that the Holy Spirit is igniting hearts with a new passion for prayer, and these prayer initiatives are seeing incredible results. I want to highlight a few of these for your encouragement and also pick out some principles we can learn from them.

24–7 Prayer

There is a growing awareness across the world of the 24–7 Prayer movement begun by Pete Greig. It started in the fall of 1999 in the United Kingdom when a group of young people, tired of being "bad" at praying, decided to pray nonstop for an entire week, 24 hours per day, passing the baton of prayer from one person to the next, so that every hour of every day was covered. They did not stop at a week, however. The week turned into a month of continuous prayer and then still continued after that. As they prayed, things began to happen: They heard angelic voices, saw numerous answers to prayer, saw many unsaved people come to their prayer room and commit their lives to Christ, and saw many worn-out Christians refreshed by God.

Almost six years later there are 24–7 Prayer rooms in sixty-three nations. Increasingly, young people around the world are looking at their own prayer lives and are becoming fascinated with the concept of unceasing prayer. As you look back through history there are a number of precedents for continuous prayer.

Why pray 24–7?

History has documented a number of prayer movements of this nature, usually preceding both great mission movements and God-encountering communities:

- Isaiah describes the "watchmen" on the walls of Jerusalem who "will never be silent day or night" (Isaiah 62:6).
- Pentecost came to a prayer room (hence the 24–7 Prayer emphasis on special rooms of prayer).
- Members of the early Church "all joined together constantly in prayer" (Acts 1:14).
- The Celtic monks at Bangor Abbey in Ireland prayed continually for 200 years, from approximately AD 559 to 759.
- The Pope decreed continual prayer in certain locations in the fifteenth century.
- In the eighteenth century a small community of Moravians began a 24–7 prayer meeting that lasted for over one hundred years and mobilized more missionaries than the Reformation.
- In Cambridge, United Kingdom, the mission movement sent out from the university emerged from the students' constant daily prayer meetings (known as the Cambridge Seven and including C. T. Studd).
- Today we know of similar movements in Seoul, Korea; Kansas, United States; and extensively throughout South America, Kenya and elsewhere.

Initially the idea for 24–7 was to dedicate one room in a church for one week of constant prayer. Now they are establishing what they call "Boiler Rooms," rooms for prayer that are open constantly and where the prayer never stops.

What is so wonderful about the 24–7 movement is that it is inspiring and mobilizing our young people to pray. If you want to inspire your young people, get them to look at the 24–7 website: www.24-7Prayer.com. It is full of creative ideas about how to pray.

Other global prayer movements and national prayer characteristics

In the northern area of Canada there is something amazing going on among the First Tribe native people. They are seeing prayer and evangelism coming together in a sweeping anointing, and there is an aspect of weeping, travailing prayer coming through the Church. People are going into the churches and finding themselves crying over the land and what has happened to it. There is a lot of reconciliation taking place. Gordon and I were involved with some people there from the Blackfoot tribe, standing with them and repenting on behalf of Britain for what our nation did in breaking our covenants concerning the First Tribe people and the Canadian lands. Different nations seem to bear different hallmarks of what God is teaching them in the place of prayer. Among the First Tribe people, God is teaching them reconciliation and tears.

In the United States God has done amazing things through The Call movement. Young people have begun to call out to God to take back cities. They have a vision to rally a call to youth and to enable "fathers to turn to their children and the children to their fathers," and for generations to stand together in their cities and begin to call on God to turn those cities around. They are setting days aside for prayer and fasting for their cities. At one rally in Washington, D.C., 400,000 young people turned up. Another took place in Boston after the 9/11 tragedy. Others have taken place in New York, Hollywood and other cities around the nation.

In South America there has been a prayer revival. God has done something there in giving people like Carlos Annacondia and Victor Lorenzo an incredible authority to confront demonic powers in cities. You can read some of their stories in books like Carlos Annacondia's *Listen to Me, Satan* (Creation House, 1998). One of the things that is needed in the West is that authority in the house of prayer. Our South American brothers and sisters can walk into a city, discern the spiritual atmosphere there and know how to confront it. God has given them a grace to pray those prayers of proclamation. They particularly have an anointing to confront the spirit of Freemasonry. They also have authority in the area of signs and wonders. I call their prayer a real "breaker" prayer. As we build our houses of prayer, we need to be open to the input of others with different anointings from us.

Ireland is a very interesting nation. There is something upon that nation that has to do with prophetic prayer and praise. There is a need for some to stand on earth and resist the enemy in prayer like the South Americans, but there is also a need for some to stand and call down the presence of God, and I believe the Irish have this anointing. They come with the song of the Lord.

All across Europe we see the idea of networking. There are city church networks developing in Norway, France and Germany. Our prayers are networked. Although each nation is quite different, we are all connected. There is a connectedness city to city, street to street; we talk to each other much more and are far more interwoven. This is Europe's strength, to mobilize a huge diversity of streams and cultures together in prayer. It is part of God's redemptive grace on Europe that He has made us networkers.

Then there is the incredible continent of Africa. I do not want to generalize too much, but I think Africa is a warrior army. There is such a spirit of warfare on the Africans. In prayer they storm heaven; they shout; they prowl around—there is a warrior spirit there, a tenacity that refuses to let go. Africans have a great capacity for prayer—they can go on for hours. They have learned a spiritual stamina and are the long-distance runners of prayer, just as they are the best long-distance runners, naturally speaking! It is part of the redemptive prayer gift God has put upon Africa.

In Africa God has put a real authority on the prayer movement to break witchcraft. They have authority because they have had to wrestle with it so much. We need their help because, much as we like to think it is not happening around us, we also have witchcraft in Europe.

In the Far East, Korea and Malaysia, we see a grace for strategic, administrative prayer. They pray in a totally different way from the rest of the world—it is very ordered and logical. In some places they will have an hour of prayer and then actually get you jumping up and down on the spot and doing some aerobics, because you are not allowed to sleep or even look vaguely sleepy in the prayer meeting! They are very quiet, not particularly aggressive like the Africans, and it is focused and meticulously planned. One of the things I have learned from Asia is the necessity for ordered, strategic prayer.

So God is bringing together this house of prayer for *all nations*. We have got our room in that house, and we also need to let the nations of the world come and teach us to pray. As prayer leaders, we need to look out for what is weak in our house of prayer. Do we need some warfare capacity? Do we need more authority? God is bringing people from all other nations to us in order to help develop our capacity for these types of prayer.

About the Author

Rachel Hickson is an internationally respected prayer leader and Bible teacher with a recognized prophetic gift. She has developed prayer and prophecy training schools in which she teaches all over the world, and is in demand as a conference speaker.

At the age of 24 Rachel entered into full-time ministry alongside Reinhard Bonnke in Africa. After just six weeks in Zimbabwe she almost lost her life in a horrific car accident, but was miraculously healed by God after intercessors prayed for her day and night. This incident birthed in Rachel a desire to pray and to help others realize the full potential of connecting with almighty God through prayer.

After returning from Africa, Rachel and her husband, Gordon, pastored a group of eight churches in North London and it was during this time that God directed them to establish Heartcry Ministries with the call to train and equip people to be released into effective prayer and intercession for their communities, cities and nations. In 2005 God called Rachel and Gordon to leave London and be based in Oxford where Gordon is associate minister on the staff of St. Aldate's Church.

Rachel travels internationally, visiting Europe, North America, Africa and India. Invitations come from various denominational backgrounds, and frequently from regional fraternals of city leaders where a passion for unity has brought the churches together to pray for a move of God in their area. Rachel and Gordon have a passion to see cities transformed through the power of prayer and evangelism. One of their projects links churches and prayer ministries across London, which has developed a city strategy called the London Prayernet (see www.londonprayer.net).

Rachel has been married to Gordon for 24 years and they have two children: their daughter, Nicola, who is married to Tim Douglass, who is on the staff of London Hillsong Church, and their son, David, who is studying at Loughborough University, United Kingdom.

Heartcry Ministries Information

Heartcry Ministries was founded in autumn 1993. The vision of Heartcry can be summarized in the following statements:

- To be one of the prophetic teaching ministries that comes alongside churches to help them understand what God is saying to them individually and corporately. To help people understand their destiny and calling, and answer the call of God in their lives.
- To train, equip and teach people and churches how to release their Heartcry to God in prayer and intercession and to be part of raising a prayer army that will cry out to God for their cities and nations.
- To provide weekend retreats, seminars and conferences in cooperation with local churches, where people can identify their hidden Heartcry, and through teaching, prayer and encouragement, find faith and healing for the restoration of their souls.
- To help people connect and answer the Heartcry of their communities. To provide prayer information and other strategies that enable the local church to connect with the Heartcry for justice, righteous government and the social needs in its city or nation.

Heartcry hopes to continue strengthening the Church and the people to hear the urgent call to prayer. Now is the time to pray and cry out for our land and continent and watch what God will do for us!

Heartcry Ministries
2 Shirelake Close
Oxford
Oxfordshire
OX1 1SN

www.heartcry.co.uk
www.londonprayer.net